On Writers & Writing

By Helen Sheehy and Leslie Stainton

Published by Tide-mark Press Ltd.

 New Moon First Quarter  Full Moon Last Quarter

Design and Typography by Corry Kaeser Cote

Catherine Drinker Bowen
(January 1, 1897 - November 1, 1973)

She felt keenly the limitations that society imposed upon women. "For many centuries," she wrote, "girls have been told that their business is wifehood, motherhood—and nothing else."

Although Bowen married and had two children, she aspired to the genderless state of the artist. "Writing saved me," she said. "The housework still had to be done ... the children still had to be followed around the yard. But these activities, repeated day after day for years, were no longer defeating because they were no longer the be-all and end-all of existence."

She drew strength from the example of her great-great-grandmother, Elizabeth Drinker, who gave birth to nine children and told her diary in 1790 that a "woman's best years came after she left off bearing and rearing."

Ironically, Bowen would achieve success and acclaim for her biographies of great male figures, including John Adams, Justice Oliver Wendell Holmes, Francis Bacon, and Benjamin Franklin. Her biography *The Lion and the Throne: The Life and Times of Sir Edward Coke* won the National Book Award in 1958. In *Biography: The Craft and the Calling* (1969), she wrote a practical, vivid guide to her art. She admired biographies that moved forward, drawing the reader into the life without "awkward hurdles, no holes to fall through. Nothing is stretched too far or condensed to the point of collapse."

One of the advantages of biography, Bowen said, was the freedom from "changing literary modes." What would she think of today's titillographers (one can't really call them biographers), whose favorite research tools are gossip, rumor, and innuendo?

Perhaps because she began her writing career as a novelist, Bowen felt that conflict, suspense, all the narrative tools of fiction were essential to good biography. She believed, however, that "the biographer finds it in history, in actual fact ... by events as they unfold, and ... by the character of the biographical subject."

She approached her subject as a lover, cherishing any word, any news. During the first months of research, she read everything she could find about her subject—getting to know his friends, his enemies, the contents of his pockets; becoming acquainted with the time, the place, even the climate; digging beneath the surface to discover the complexity of the human being. "Love comes slowly," she warned, "after deep acquaintance and many arguments back and forth."

Writing biography changed her life. "One has climbed a hill," she said, "looked out and over, and the valley of one's own condition will be forever greener."

Sunday
29

Monday
30

Tuesday
31

 *Wednesday*
1

Catherine Drinker Bowen, b. 1897
New Year's Day

Thursday
2

Friday
3

Saturday
4

December 1996						
S	**M**	**T**	**W**	**T**	**F**	**S**
1	2	3	4	5	6	7
8	9	10	11	12	13	14
15	16	17	18	19	20	21
22	23	24	25	26	27	28
29	30	31				

January
1997

February						
S	**M**	**T**	**W**	**T**	**F**	**S**
						1
2	3	4	5	6	7	8
9	10	11	12	13	14	15
16	17	18	19	20	21	22
23	24	25	26	27	28	

Sunday
5

Monday
6

Carl Sandburg, b. 1878

Tuesday
7

Zora Neale Hurston, b. 1891

Wednesday
8

Wilkie Collins, b. 1824

Thursday
9

Friday
10

Ramadan begins

Saturday
11
Jack London, b. 1876   Alan Paton, b. 1903

December 1996										
S	M	T	W	T	F	S
1	2	3	4	5	6	7
8	9	10	11	12	13	14
15	16	17	18	19	20	21
22	23	24	25	26	27	28
29	30	31				

January
1997

February						
S	M	T	W	T	F	S
						1
2	3	4	5	6	7	8
9	10	11	12	13	14	15
16	17	18	19	20	21	22
23	24	25	26	27	28	

Alan Paton
(January 11, 1903 - April 12, 1988)

On September 24, 1946, Alan Paton, principal of the Diepkloof Reformatory in South Africa, toured Trondheim Cathedral in Norway. At the end of the tour, he sat in a front pew opposite the rose window. "The light was shining behind it," he recalled. "I was in the grip of powerful emotion ... filled with an intense homesickness, for ... wife and sons ... and my far-off country." When he returned to his hotel room at six that day, Paton wrote the first sentences of *Cry, the Beloved Country*. "There is a lovely road that runs from Ixopo into the hills. These hills are grass-covered and rolling, and they are lovely beyond any singing of it."

For the next three months as he visited prisons, schools, and institutions in Norway, England, and America, Paton worked on his novel. "My energy seemed endless," he said. "Above all I tried to make a story, not a denunciation or a sermon or a lesson ... if you want to tell a story you must go to the desk and obey the rules of the craft." After reading six chapters, Maxwell Perkins of Charles Scribner's Sons accepted the book, and for once Perkins had no use for his legendary editorial skill. He did not suggest any changes, additions, or alterations.

Only the Bible has outsold *Cry, the Beloved Country* in South Africa. Since its publication in 1948, the novel has sold more than 15 million copies in 20 languages. Sidney Poitier starred in the movie, and *Lost in the Stars*, a Broadway musical based on the book, opened in 1952.

"I had an eye on my fellow white South Africans and white Americans when I wrote the book," said Paton. In the same year that *Cry, the Beloved Country* was published, the Nationalist Party gained power in South Africa and instituted the system of apartheid. In 1953, Paton became president of the Liberal Party of South Africa. For the rest of his life, Paton championed justice and democracy there.

Raised by an abusive father, Paton had learned early on that "physical force never achieved anything but a useless obedience." Paton abhorred authoritarianism in any form. At Diepkloof Reformatory he took down the barbed wire and planted geraniums. He was known for his iron will. "Some would call it courage," he said. "Some would call it inordinate pride. I myself call it stubbornness."

Just before he died, even as violence and conflict in South Africa were on the rise, Paton told a reporter, "I still believe there is hope."

Horatio Alger, Jr.
(January 13, 1832 - July 18, 1899)

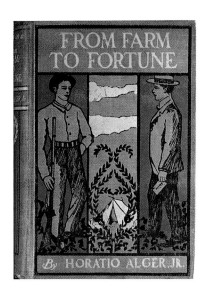

His first biographer felt that Horatio Alger's life was so dull and colorless that he titled his book *A Biography Without a Hero*. Alger didn't drink, smoke, gamble, or carouse with women, but he was the hero of his own life, and if his hidden history could be uncovered, it might make a tale as gripping as one of his own thrilling plots.

Horatio Alger wrote over 130 books which sold approximately 20 million copies. For 30 years, from 1868 until 1899, Horatio Alger's serial books for boys were the most popular books of the time. *Ragged Dick*, *Luck and Pluck*, and *Tattered Tom* told the tales of boys who struggled against poverty and misfortune, but who overcame all obstacles to become happy and wealthy.

Born in Revere, Massachusetts, into a religious Puritan family, Horatio was a slight, delicate child, nicknamed "Holy Horatio" by his fellows. His stern, minister father pressed him to enter the ministry, and after graduating from Harvard, Alger attended divinity school. He wanted to be a writer, though, and he began to write stories and poems which were published in magazines and newspapers. In 1864, Alger became a minister, but he resigned the pulpit in 1866 under a cloud of suspicion about "questionable relations" with the choirboys. He moved to New York City where he would spend the rest of his life.

Alger could have afforded to live in an uptown mansion, but he chose to live in boardinghouses similar to the lodgings of his fictional heroes. His second home was the Newsboy's Lodging House, a refuge for boys who flocked to the city to find work. Alger wrote there, took his meals there, and sometimes even slept in the dormitories. The superintendent of the school and the boys revered Alger. He often used the real names of the newsboys and drew on their experiences in his serials. Many of his books are dedicated to the boys he befriended. He gave them money and gifts, paid for magazine subscriptions and books, and he maintained a voluminous correspondence long after they became grown men.

During his writing life, Alger earned almost a million dollars from his books, but he died penniless because he gave most of his income away. Alger's appeal was so great that his name earned money even after his death. Edward Stratemeyer, who wrote the Rover Boys books, published 11 books under Alger's name. The name Horatio Alger has become a household word, a symbol of success.

Sunday
12

Monday
13

Horatio Alger, Jr., b. 1832
Tuesday
14

Yukio Mishima, b. 1925
 Wednesday
15

Molière, b. 1622
Thursday
16

Friday
17

Anne Brontë, b. 1820
Don Pedro Calderón de la Barca b. 1600
Saturday
18
A. A. Milne, b. 1882

December 1996						
S	**M**	**T**	**W**	**T**	**F**	**S**
1	2	3	4	5	6	7
8	9	10	11	12	13	14
15	16	17	18	19	20	21
22	23	24	25	26	27	28
29	30	31				

January
1997

February						
S	**M**	**T**	**W**	**T**	**F**	**S**
						1
2	3	4	5	6	7	8
9	10	11	12	13	14	15
16	17	18	19	20	21	22
23	24	25	26	27	28	

Sunday
19
Edgar Allan Poe, b. 1809

Monday
20

Richard Le Gallienne, b. 1866
Wellington Anniversary (N.Z.)
Martin Luther King, Jr. Day

Tuesday
21

Wednesday
22

George Gordon, Lord Byron, b. 1788

Thursday
23

Friday
24

Edith Wharton, b. 1862

Saturday
25
Virgina Woolf, b. 1882

December 1996						
S	M	T	W	T	F	S
1	2	3	4	5	6	7
8	9	10	11	12	13	14
15	16	17	18	19	20	21
22	23	24	25	26	27	28
29	30	31				

January
1997

February						
S	M	T	W	T	F	S
						1
2	3	4	5	6	7	8
9	10	11	12	13	14	15
16	17	18	19	20	21	22
23	24	25	26	27	28	

Edith Wharton

(January 24, 1862 - August 11, 1937)

Van Wyck Brooks recalled her "cold stare."
F. Scott Fitzgerald accused her of knowing
nothing of life. Edith Wharton, the author of
46 volumes, including novels, short stories,
and essays, designer of houses and gardens,
an arbiter of taste, and friend to the famous,
seemed a formidable figure to a younger
generation of writers.

As a child, she was not allowed to read any
new fiction. Instead she read Keats, Shelley,
Shakespeare, the Bible. Alone in her library,
she felt "a secret ecstasy of communion."

She began writing in childhood, scribbling
her stories on brown wrapping paper. She
said that her early stories were the "excess
of youth ... all written at the top of my voice."
Even later, when she read one of her books in proof, she said, "With all my trying I
can't write yet. ... There isn't a single sentence in the book with natural magic in it—
not an inevitable phrase." The process of writing *The House of Mirth* in 1903 and
1904 transformed her, she said, from "a drifting amateur into a professional" and
taught her the "discipline of the daily task." In 1921 she won the Pulitzer Prize for
The Age of Innocence—the first woman to receive that award.

In 1922 Wharton read James Joyce's *Ulysses* and thought it was adolescent drivel. She
found T. S. Eliot's *The Wasteland* cold and lifeless. The success of their work, though,
made her feel like "a deplorable example of what people used to read in the Dark
Ages." Male authors didn't understand a woman's sexual feelings, she felt, and in an
unpublished piece titled "Beatrice Palmato," Wharton proved that she could write
explicitly and sensuously about physical passion.

Her own favorite author was George Sand. Like Sand, Wharton lived for many years
in Paris. She moved there partly to free herself from her disastrous marriage with
Edward "Teddy" Wharton. In her mid-40s, while she was still married, Wharton fell
passionately in love with journalist Morton Fullerton, who said that Edith "displayed
the reckless ardor of a George Sand."

In his monumental biography of Wharton, R. W. B. Lewis revealed the artist and the
woman. It was her writings, he concluded, that "constituted the life she had most truly
and deeply lived ... the men and women she had loved, seemed to her increasingly to
be creatures of fiction, parts of some other narrative she had yet to compose."

"I have wondered," wrote Lewis, "whether her reputation might today stand even
higher if she had been a man."

Thomas Paine
(January 29, 1737 - June 8, 1809)

Thomas Paine's political consciousness was born early. He grew up in a small town in England where criminals—most of them poor—were hanged each spring within a stone's throw of his house. That grisly spectacle, and what it said about Britain's class structure, fostered Paine's hatred of social injustice and helped spark his desire to emigrate.

After a brief education in grammar school, Paine worked, in turn, as a corset-maker, sailor, teacher, and tax collector before going broke and electing to move to America. He arrived in Philadelphia in 1774, at the age of 37, with a letter of introduction from Benjamin Franklin,

THOMAS PAINE.

whom he'd met the previous year in London. Franklin's letter identified him as a worthy young man suitable for employment as "a clerk, or assistant tutor in a school, or assistant surveyor."

Thanks to circumstance, he became much more. Within five months of Paine's arrival in America, Thomas Jefferson had drafted the Declaration of Independence and Paine had found the cause he needed in order to make his mark. In January, 1776, he published what has since become one of America's most significant political documents, the essay *Common Sense*. In simple, forthright, persuasive language Paine argued the cause of American independence and urged his fellow colonists to embrace revolution. Galvanized by the essay, they did.

"It was the cause of America that made me an author," Paine said afterward. The success of *Common Sense* catapulted him into fame and prompted him to keep writing. In later years he put his pen to work arguing for revolution in France and reform in England.

But his heart remained with America, the only "real republic." He spent his last years in New York state, a smelly, incontinent, often drunk old man whose nails grew so long they curled around his toes. Always obstinate, often rude, Paine offended many in his long life. At his death, the Quaker church refused him a burial plot. He was interred instead on a local farm. Among the few to attend his burial were a French woman and her son, who stood at either end of his grave throughout the service. "Oh! Mr. Paine!" the woman exclaimed as earth fell onto the coffin. "My son stands here as testimony of the gratitude of America, and I, for France."

Sunday
26

Monday
27

Lewis Carroll, b. 1832
Auckland Anniversary (N.Z.)

Tuesday
28

Sidonie-Gabrielle Colette, b. 1873

Wednesday
29

Thomas Paine, b.1737
Anton Chekhov, b. 1860

Thursday
30

 Friday
31

Zane Grey, b. 1872
Freya Stark, b. 1893

Saturday
1

December 1996						
S	M	T	W	T	F	S
1	2	3	4	5	6	7
8	9	10	11	12	13	14
15	16	17	18	19	20	21
22	23	24	25	26	27	28
29	30	31				

January/February
1997

February						
S	M	T	W	T	F	S
						1
2	3	4	5	6	7	8
9	10	11	12	13	14	15
16	17	18	19	20	21	22
23	24	25	26	27	28	

Sunday
2
Ayn Rand, b. 1905

Monday
3

Gertrude Stein, b. 1874

Tuesday
4

Wednesday
5

Thursday
6

Christopher Marlowe, b. 1564
Waitangi Day (N.Z.)

Friday
7

Charles Dickens, b. 1812   Laura Ingalls Wilder, b. 1867

Saturday
8
Eid-al-Fitr   *Kate Chopin, b. 1850*

January						
S	M	T	W	T	F	S
				1	2	3	4
5	6	7	8	9	10	11
12	13	14	15	16	17	18
19	20	21	22	23	24	25
26	27	28	29	30	31	

February
1997

March						
S	M	T	W	T	F	S
						1
2	3	4	5	6	7	8
9	10	11	12	13	14	15
16	17	18	19	20	21	22
23	24	25	26	27	28	29
30	31					

Charles Dickens
(February 7, 1812 - June 9, 1870)

When Charles Dickens visited America in 1842, dour Boston intellectuals sneered at his flamboyant red waistcoat, his unkempt black hair, and his "dissipated looking mouth." Still, they marveled at the writer's cleverness. " Take the genius out of his face," one observer sniped, "and there are a thousand young London shop-keepers ... who look exactly like him."

None of his family, including his wastrel of a father, suspected Charles Dickens' genius. When his father was imprisoned for failure to pay his debts, 12-year-old Charles gave up his dream of going to school; instead he toiled in Warren's Blacking Warehouse pasting paper labels

onto pots of shoe polish. His father's imprisonment and the loss of his childhood embittered Dickens, but the humiliations he suffered inspired his art, including his own favorite novel, the autobiographical *David Copperfield*.

Trained first as a court reporter and journalist, Dickens captured and criticized the social reality of his time. On his trip to America, he toured factories, prisons, and insane asylums. He knew London's darkest streets, and whenever he visited Paris he was "dragged by invisible force into the Morgue ... with its ghastly beds, and the swollen saturated clothes hanging up, and the water dripping, dripping all day long, upon that other swollen saturated something in the corner, like a heap of crushed over-ripe figs."

Dickens packed telling details of gritty life into his books, but, influenced by his two favorite authors, Shakespeare and Goldsmith, he also wrote with theatrical flair, creating eccentric, timeless characters. Many of his books, like *Oliver Twist*, *Nicholas Nickleby*, *A Christmas Carol*, *A Tale of Two Cities*, and *Great Expectations*, have become stage plays and movies. Dickens usually wrote from nine to three every day, and when he finished he rushed outside to "take fierce exercise, the pen once laid down is leaden—and not feathery."

In his books, Dickens often idealized and sentimentalized family life. His own domestic situation was far from ideal. The father of ten children, Dickens called himself a "misplaced and mismarried man," and in his middle age he created a scandal when he separated from his wife and found happiness with a young actress.

Derided at times for sentimentality (Oscar Wilde quipped that "one must have a heart of stone to read the death of *Little Nell* ... without laughing"), Dickens entertained and educated readers of every social class, and his books were read aloud to illiterates. Today, Dickens is surpassed only by Shakespeare in popularity and affection.

Boris Pasternak
(February 10, 1890 - May 30, 1960)

To Boris Pasternak, a book was "a cube-shaped chunk of blazing, smoking conscience—nothing more."

"Compose a novel about our epoch," a friend had told him, "freshen it with our great reality." When he was young, Pasternak yearned to write a "big novel: with love." Although it took him 40 years to write *Doctor Zhivago*, he wrote the novel with "great ease," he reported. "The circumstances were so definite, so fabulously terrible. All that I had to do was listen to their prompting with my whole soul and follow obediently their suggestions."

Born to artistic parents—his mother was a concert pianist and his father was a portrait painter—Pasternak studied music as a boy. A collection of poems by Rainer Maria Rilke, a small book of verse with a faded, gray cover that fell by chance from a bookcase into Pasternak's hands, inspired him. In 1909, he gave up music to write poetry and study philosophy at the University of Moscow. His first poetry collection, *Twin in the Clouds*, was published in 1914. From 1915 to 1917, unable to serve in the army because of a broken leg, he worked on a draft board in the Urals.

At first, Pasternak believed in the Bolshevik Revolution. He was soon disillusioned by the restrictions on artistic freedom, however. He married and lived for a few years in Germany, but he returned to Moscow in 1923 after the revolution. During Stalin's reign of terror and the purges of the 1930s, Pasternak practiced "the genre of silence." Unable to publish his original poetry and prose, he translated Goethe, Shakespeare, and English poetry. Despite continued harassment and persecution by the government, he managed to complete *Doctor Zhivago*. The book was published in Italy in 1956, translated widely, and was acclaimed around the world. In 1958, Pasternak won the Nobel Prize. "For me this is more than just a joy; it is a moral support," he said. Pasternak thought of himself as an avenger for all those who had suffered under the repressive Soviet regime. When Soviet authorities threatened his family and friends, Pasternak was forced to give up the award.

"I stand alone," wrote Yuri Zhivago in one of his poems. "All else is swamped by Pharisaism. To live life to the end is not a childish task." Pasternak, the creator of the doctor/poet Zhivago and the unforgettable Lara, spent his last years in exile in a writers' community outside Moscow. When he died in 1960, thousands gathered in the streets of Moscow to honor his artistry and his moral courage.

Sunday

9

Amy Lowell, b. 1874

Monday

10

Bertolt Brecht, b. 1898   *Boris Pasternak, b. 1890*

Tuesday

11

Shrove Tuesday

Wednesday

12

Charles Darwin, b. 1809
Abraham Lincoln, born 1809
Ash Wednesday

Thursday

13

 Friday

14

St. Valentine's Day

Saturday

15

January						
S	**M**	**T**	**W**	**T**	**F**	**S**
			1	2	3	4
5	6	7	8	9	10	11
12	13	14	15	16	17	18
19	20	21	22	23	24	25
26	27	28	29	30	31	

February
1997

March						
S	**M**	**T**	**W**	**T**	**F**	**S**
						1
2	3	4	5	6	7	8
9	10	11	12	13	14	15
16	17	18	19	20	21	22
23	24	25	26	27	28	29
30	31					

Sunday
16

Monday
17

Tuesday
18

Wednesday
19

Carson McCullers, b. 1917

Thursday
20

Friday
21

Anaïs Nin, b. 1903

Saturday
22

George Washington, born 1732   *Edna St. Vincent Millay, b. 1892*

January						
S	M	T	W	T	F	S
				1	2	3	4
5	6	7	8	9	10	11
12	13	14	15	16	17	18
19	20	21	22	23	24	25
26	27	28	29	30	31	

February
1997

March						
S	M	T	W	T	F	S
						1
2	3	4	5	6	7	8
9	10	11	12	13	14	15
16	17	18	19	20	21	22
23	24	25	26	27	28	29
30	31					

Anaïs Nin
(February 21, 1903 - January 14, 1977)

Wherever she went, she carried her
journal with her. She wrote in it while
waiting for friends at cafés, while having
her hair washed, at train stations and bus
depots, on journeys, during dull lectures
at the Sorbonne, "almost while people
are talking," she confessed. Her diary
was Anaïs Nin's refuge and vice, "my
kief, hashish, and opium pipe." She
craved it as others crave food or wine
or drugs. "The period without the
diary," she said, "remains an ordeal."

Her friends in Paris urged Nin to move
from the diary to other forms of literature,
and from time to time she did. In 1932 she published a short critical study of D. H.
Lawrence, a man whose work and ideals she revered; Nin later claimed to have
written the book in just 16 days. She wrote a handful of novels and prose poems,
and in the 1940s she cranked out a collection of erotica for a patron who paid her
$1 a page for sexually explicit material. "Less poetry," he said after he'd seen her
first efforts. "Be specific." Nin ignored him and produced her own brand of
explicit but elegant prose. Years later, the collection became a bestseller.

But her passion was her diary. She began the work when she was eleven, after her
father, Joaquín, a Spanish pianist and composer, had deserted his family, and Nin's
mother, Rosa, a French-Dane, had moved with her three children from their native
France to New York. Anaïs started the journal in an attempt to recover her father,
but the endeavor soon took on a life of its own and became a way of pursuing and
articulating herself.

She was never private about the diary. Few such works, in fact, have been more
relentlessly self-promoted. Her friends knew she was writing it, and many asked her
not to report in it what they said or did. Her close friend Henry Miller, however, often
told her to "put this down in your diary."

In everything she wrote, Nin explored the inner life, particularly the inner life of
women. She observed that the writer's role was "not to say what we can all say, but
what we are unable to say." Keenly influenced by Surrealism and by the work of Carl
Jung, she believed that one must "proceed from the dream outward." Describing the
role of the diary in her life, she once said, "Instead of writing a novel, I lie back with
this book and a pen, and dream."

Rosalía de Castro
(February 24, 1837 - July 15, 1885)

The odds were against her. First, she was a woman. Second, she was born and raised in one of the most backward regions of Spain. Third, she was the illegitimate daughter of a priest.

Rosalía de Castro once remarked that women were born "only to endure as many hardships as can be inflicted on the weakest, most delicate part of humanity." Her own brief life bore witness to her conviction. She married a man who later proved unfaithful to her. Of the seven children they had together, two died before the age of two. Because of the circumstances of her birth, Rosalía de Castro never achieved respectability among her bourgeois neighbors in Santiago de Compostela, and because they were both writers, neither she nor her husband ever had money.

Through eyes tempered by sorrow, she registered the sorrow of others: peasants from her native Galicia who came begging in the cities when famine struck the countryside; a friend who succumbed to typhus in her youth; women condemned to a lifetime of drudgery and the "uncertainties of hope, the blackness of solitude, the anguish of a perennial misery."

In poems and novels Castro gave voice to the difficulties she both endured and saw, and at the same time she exalted the "eternally green countryside" and "eternally beautiful beaches" of Galicia, a region known as much for its poverty as for its charms.

Castro published her first book of poems when she was 20. Two years later, she brought out her first novel and also gave birth to her first child. More children and books followed. Although she wrote both poetry and prose, it was poetry for which Castro became celebrated, in particular her 1863 collection *Cantares gallegas*, an assortment of poems inspired by the music and lyrics of popular Galician songs and written in Galician, a venerable language of northwestern Spain. The book transcended regional boundaries and helped elevate Castro to her current status as one of the foremost postromantic poets of 19th-century Spain.

Like her more famous American contemporary, Emily Dickinson, Castro wrote of nature, death, time, and longing. Her muse, she said, was sadness. A heavy, awkward woman, Castro once declined to give her photograph to a newspaper reporter who requested it. "Women such as I, who have not received the splendid gifts of physical beauty from nature, must be excused from exposing their faces to public view," she said. Castro died at age 48 and is buried in Santiago, the damp, gray town of her birth, a city whose beauty she never ceased to cherish.

W.E.B. Du Bois, b. 1868   Samuel Pepys, b. 1633

Monday
24

Rosalía de Castro, b. 1837

Tuesday
25

Carlo Goldoni, b. 1707

Wednesday
26

Victor Hugo, b. 1802

Thursday
27

Henry Wadsworth Longfellow, b. 1807
John Steinbeck, b. 1902

Friday
28

Michel de Montaigne, b. 1533

Saturday
1

January						
S	M	T	W	T	F	S
			1	2	3	4
5	6	7	8	9	10	11
12	13	14	15	16	17	18
19	20	21	22	23	24	25
26	27	28	29	30	31	

February/March
1997

March						
S	M	T	W	T	F	S
						1
2	3	4	5	6	7	8
9	10	11	12	13	14	15
16	17	18	19	20	21	22
23	24	25	26	27	28	29
30	31					

Sunday
2

Camille Desmoulins, b. 1760

Monday
3

Tuesday
4

Wednesday
5

Constance Fenimore Woolson, b. 1840

Thursday
6

Elizabeth Barrett Browning, b. 1806
Ring Lardner, b. 1885

Friday
7

Saturday
8

February						
S	M	T	W	T	F	S
						1
2	3	4	5	6	7	8
9	10	11	12	13	14	15
16	17	18	19	20	21	22
23	24	25	26	27	28	

March
1997

April						
S	M	T	W	T	F	S
		1	2	3	4	5
6	7	8	9	10	11	12
13	14	15	16	17	18	19
20	21	22	23	24	25	26
27	28	29	30			

Camille Desmoulins
(March 2, 1760 - April 5, 1794)

Baptized Lucie-Simplice-Amille-Benoist, the journalist and patriot Camille Desmoulins years later asked his father, "Did you guess that I should be a Roman when you christened me Lucius, Sulpicius, Camillus?"

The ideals, rhetoric, and sensibility of ancient Rome—a key part of his schooling in Paris as a boy—informed most of what Camille Desmoulins believed and preached in his short, passionate life. From the heroes of the Roman Republic he learned to value courage and frugality, and from its orators, notably Cicero, he learned to write.

Desmoulins became his own hero on Sunday, July 12, 1789, two days before his fellow Parisians stormed the Bastille. Swept up in the revolutionary currents of the day, the 29-year-old lawyer and sometime poet leapt onto a café table in the crowded Palais-Royal that Sunday afternoon and delivered the speech of his life. Hair spilling onto his shoulders, Desmoulins shouted to his fellow citizens to take up arms against the monarchy. "Yes, yes, it is I who call my brothers to freedom," he cried, waving a pistol in one hand. "I would die rather than submit to servitude."

The speech transformed Desmoulins from a struggling, unknown lawyer into an idol of Paris. Days later he published an incendiary pamphlet reiterating his call to arms. By September of 1789, he was famous. "One no longer says 'it's a pamphlet by an author named Desmoulins,'" he told his father, "but 'it's a pamphlet by Desmoulins.'" Later that year he launched the first in a series of news-sheets entitled *Révolutions de France et de Brabant* and written exclusively by Desmoulins. With their elegant prose and deadly wit, the weekly sheets established Desmoulins as a key figure in the French Revolution and one of the greatest journalists of his age.

Desmoulins once described himself as a "weathercock" who shifted as the wind shifts. In the years following the seizure of the Bastille, he used his pen at first to foment revolution and then, during the dreadful time of the Terror, to question the tactics of its leaders.

In the end, Desmoulins himself fell victim to the revolution he had helped to spark. Accused of supporting the counter-revolution, he was arrested in March 1794, tried, and sentenced to death. As he awaited his execution, he wrote to his wife from jail. "I dreamt of a revolution that everyone would embrace," he told her. "I could not have believed men would be capable of such cruelty, of such injustice."

The Healing Power of Literature

The inscription on the door of the library at ancient Thebes bore this simple motto: "Medicine for the soul."

Literature has long had the strength to heal. Aristotle praised its cathartic powers. Centuries later an ailing John Stuart Mill found in the poetry of Wordsworth "a medicine for my state of mind," and Helen Keller—afflicted from birth by multiple disabilities—discovered, by reading Homer's *Iliad*, that she was "conscious of a soul-sense that lifts me above the narrow, cramping circumstances of my life."

Sick people, wrote critic Anatole Broyard in the midst of his struggle with cancer, "need a literature of their own. Misery loves company—if it's good company." Broyard identified a handful of great books on the subject of illness: Tolstoy's *Death of Ivan Ilyich*, most of Kafka, Malcom Lowry's *Under the Volcano*, and Thomas Mann's *Magic Mountain*—"the grand, definitive portrait of illness"—in which a tubercular woman gives her physician-lover an x-ray of her lungs as a remembrance of their first and only night together.

Disease inspired Boccaccio to create *The Decameron*, Keats to write the "Ode to a Nightingale," and John Donne to compose his *Devotions upon Emergent Occasions*. It forced Michel de Montaigne to retreat to a castle where he could do little but write, and it drove Thomas De Quincey to take opium, which in turn led to his eloquent *Confessions of an Opium Eater*.

Plagued by psychiatric illness, Heinrich Heine credited disease with having fostered the creation which was "my body's purge, / Creating I've grown sane and sound." Graham Greene likewise found writing to be a form of therapy by which he could escape "the madness, the melancholia, the panic fear which is inherent in the human situation."

Disease, and those who treat it, prompted Voltaire, Shaw, and Flannery O'Connor to rail against doctors. But for sheer vitriol, no writer has surpassed Molière, who in one of his plays asked, "Why does he need four doctors—is not one enough to kill a patient?"

More sympathetic was Anton Chekhov, himself a physician, who defined medicine as his "lawful wife" and literature as his "mistress." Chekhov claimed that his work in medicine broadened his observations, deepened his knowledge, and steeled him against illusions. His fellow doctor-writer, William Carlos Williams, found poetry in "the half-spoken words of such patients as the physician sees from day to day."

Of the timeless bond between literature and health, Dr. Johnson had this to say: "The only end of writing is to enable readers better to enjoy life or better to endure it."

Sunday

9

Vita Sackville-West, b. 1892   Mothering Sunday (U.K.)

Monday

10

Tuesday

11

Wednesday

12

Jack Kerouac, b. 1922
Gabriele D'Annunzio, b. 1863

Thursday

13

Janet Flanner, b. 1892

Friday

14

 Saturday

15

Lady Gregory, b. 1852   *Richard Ellmann, b. 1918*

February						
S	M	T	W	T	F	S
						1
2	3	4	5	6	7	8
9	10	11	12	13	14	15
16	17	18	19	20	21	22
23	24	25	26	27	28	

March
1997

April						
S	M	T	W	T	F	S
		1	2	3	4	5
6	7	8	9	10	11	12
13	14	15	16	17	18	19
20	21	22	23	24	25	26
27	28	29	30			

Sunday
16

Monday
17

St. Patrick's Day   *Kate Greenaway, b. 1846*

Tuesday
18

Wednesday
19

Thursday
20

Ovid, b. 43 B.C.
Henrik Ibsen, b. 1828
Friedrich Hölderlin, b. 1770
Nikolai Gogol, b. 1809
Spring Equinox, 8:56 am EST

Friday
21

Saturday
22

February						
S	M	T	W	T	F	S
						1
2	3	4	5	6	7	8
9	10	11	12	13	14	15
16	17	18	19	20	21	22
23	24	25	26	27	28	

March
1997

April						
S	M	T	W	T	F	S
		1	2	3	4	5
6	7	8	9	10	11	12
13	14	15	16	17	18	19
20	21	22	23	24	25	26
27	28	29	30			

Kate Greenaway
(March 17, 1846 - November 6, 1901)

In some ways Kate Greenaway remained a child throughout her life. "I hated to be grown-up, and cried when I had my first long dress," she remembered.

She was plain, introspective, and shy. She disliked school. On nights when she could not sleep, she often left her bed to go and watch her father, an illustrator, engrave woodblocks. In the morning she would cook her father breakfast and give her opinion of the finished block. She had an acute eye for detail and a sharp desire to learn, and he welcomed her advice.

Despite her failures at school, Kate soon realized that she could succeed at tasks if she approached them at her own pace. She became enamored of illustrated books and periodicals—so much so that unless the illustrations for a given book failed to convey its story, she never bothered to read the text. When she was 12 her father enrolled her in art school. By the time she reached 27, she had established a thriving career as a greeting card designer.

At 29 she published her first book, *Under the Window*, a collection of "coloured pictures and rhymes for children" in which Greenaway recalled the charmed world of her own Victorian girlhood. One reviewer observed that children would delight in the book's pretty pictures, while adults would relish "... the grace of an unconscious childhood."

With the publication of this and dozens of subsequent books—including *Mother Goose, The Language of Flowers, A Apple Pie*, and a yearly series of almanacs—Greenaway's reputation soared. In 1881 *The New York Times* pronounced her the best children's book illustrator of her time. Mostly, however, she illustrated other people's books—not her own. She longed to be a poet, and towards the end of her life she devoted herself to that aim, filling hundreds of handwritten pages with her verse.

For most of her adult life, Greenaway was passionately in love with the art critic John Ruskin. But Ruskin never returned her love as she hoped. In her sadness, Greenaway turned to memories of her childhood, and those memories gave her joy. In her drawings and poems she rendered that Arcadian world time and again. "I had such a very happy time when I was a child," she said once. "I had days of gloom—sometimes—but I believe even those were so strong as to be a satisfaction to me."

Fannie Merritt Farmer
(March 23, 1857 - January 15, 1915)

She was not the best cook in the Farmer family. Her younger sister May was more adept in the kitchen, and the household maid, Maggie Murphy, produced better pastries and chowders. Fannie was apt to let the pots burn as she dashed from one recipe to the next.

It was ironic, then, that she should become the principal of the Boston Cooking School, the author of a best-selling cookbook, and a woman widely considered "the finest cook in the country."

Even her publisher, Little Brown, was skeptical when Fannie Merritt Farmer first approached them with the collection of recipes that later became the *Boston Cooking School Cook Book*. Only with misgivings—and only at Farmer's expense—did the firm agree to publish the book. A cautious 3,000 copies appeared in 1896. To Little Brown's astonishment, the public devoured them. Before long,

An illustration from the 1937 edition of the *Boston Cooking School Cook Book*

sales of Fannie Farmer's cookbook had outstripped those of the publisher's two best-selling works, *Quo Vadis?* and *Little Women*. Eventually Farmer's book settled down to an average sum of 50,000 sales a year.

American cooks found recipes for everything from Baked Ham with Champagne Sauce to Poor Man's Pudding in Farmer's compendium. Scattered throughout the book were bits of homely advice—"To bake is to cook in an oven"—as well as evidence of Farmer's most ingenious contribution to the science of cookery, level measurements.

She wrote the book, at age 38, using the recipes her family had accumulated during decades of mouth-watering culinary experimentation. Pacing up and down the crowded parlor of her family's Boston home, her red hair piled high on her head, Farmer dictated the 700-page book to her sister Cora, who sat at a table, taking down notes with a fine pen.

As a writer, Fannie Farmer was obsessed with her subject. In her quest for new recipes to fill subsequent editions of her cookbook, she took research trips to nearby towns and faraway cities. Confronted by chefs who refused to yield the secrets of their kitchens, Farmer guessed at ingredients. According to one admirer, she had "a Sherlockian tongue."

A dedicated teacher as well as writer, Farmer remained devoted to her craft. When a stroke left her paralyzed at the age of 51, she taught from a wheelchair. She gave her final lecture just ten days before her death at the age of 58. After her death, the *Boston Cooking School Cook Book* stayed in the Farmer family and eventually became the *Fannie Farmer Cook Book*. It has never been out of print.

Sunday
23

Fannie Merritt Farmer, b. 1857   Palm Sunday

Monday
24

Olive Schreiner, b. 1855
Otago & Southland Anniversary (N.Z.)

Tuesday
25

Flannery O'Connor, b. 1925

Wednesday
26

Robert Frost, b. 1874
Tennessee Williams, b. 1911

Thursday
27

Friday
28

Maxim Gorky, b. (Gregorian calendar) 1928
Easter Friday (N.Z.)
Good Friday

Saturday
29

February						
S	**M**	**T**	**W**	**T**	**F**	**S**
						1
2	3	4	5	6	7	8
9	10	11	12	13	14	15
16	17	18	19	20	21	22
23	24	25	26	27	28	

March
1997

April						
S	**M**	**T**	**W**	**T**	**F**	**S**
		1	2	3	4	5
6	7	8	9	10	11	12
13	14	15	16	17	18	19
20	21	22	23	24	25	26
27	28	29	30			

Sunday
30
Easter   *Sean O'Casey, b. 1880*

Monday
31

Andrew Marvell, b. 1621
Easter Monday (Canada, U.K., N.Z.)

Tuesday
1

Matsuo Basho, b. 1644
Edmond Rostand, b. 1868

Wednesday
2

H. C. Andersen, b. 1805
Giacomo Girolamo Casanova, b. 1725

Thursday
3

Washington Irving, b. 1783

Friday
4

Saturday
5

February						
S	M	T	W	T	F	S
						1
2	3	4	5	6	7	8
9	10	11	12	13	14	15
16	17	18	19	20	21	22
23	24	25	26	27	28	

March/April
1997

April						
S	M	T	W	T	F	S
		1	2	3	4	5
6	7	8	9	10	11	12
13	14	15	16	17	18	19
20	21	22	23	24	25	26
27	28	29	30			

Andrew Marvell
(March 31, 1621 - August 16, 1678)

What little we know about Andrew
Marvell's life is due more to politics
than to poetry. Marvell satirized the
court, defended Cromwell, served as
a diplomat under Charles II, and ended
his days as a member of Parliament from
the city of Hull. (During his first session
of Parliament he got into a fistfight.) His
life is frustrating, says poet Donald Hall,
one of Marvell's most ardent fans, "for
the poet inside the MP remains elusive."

During his lifetime Marvell published
few poems, and none for which he is
remembered today. Poetry, in fact, seems
to have been a minor part of what he did.

He wrote some of his best verse while working as a tutor for the daughter of one of
Cromwell's generals. Other poems were occasioned by political circumstance, and
still others—including a series on mowers and gardens—by whimsy.

Marvell could turn the slightest of themes into a source of profound complexity. T. S.
Eliot, whose classic 1921 essay on Marvell helped rescue the poet from the ranks of
the second-rate, praised Marvell's ability to take "a slight thing"—a girl's devotion
to her pet fawn, for example—and give it "a connection with that inexhaustible and
terrible nebula of emotion which surrounds all our exact and practical passions."

A skilled linguist, Marvell wrote many of his poems in Latin and at least one in Greek.
But he turned to English for his most famous poem, "To His Coy Mistress," a genial
reworking of the timeworn carpe diem theme. With his characteristic wit, Marvell
urged the "coy" lady of his title to relinquish her "long-preserved virginity" before
her honor turns "to dust; / And into ashes all my lust."

Marvell himself never married. At one point during his life his political adversaries
denounced him as a homosexual, and they may have been telling the truth. After his
death, a volume of Marvell's poems appeared with a preface by a woman claiming
to be the author's widow. The mysterious "Mary Marvell" turned out to be the poet's
housekeeper. Had she been Marvell's widow, she could have laid claim to monies
from his estate.

For decades after his death, Marvell was best remembered as a lover of liberty, not
as a creator of poetry. And yet his work has inspired poets from Dryden to Pope to
Eliot to Hall. In his great poems, writes Hall, Marvell "always uses meter to think
aloud in. ... Poetry is a language for thinking aloud in—and not for putting thoughts
into words."

Matsuo Bashō
(1644? - 1694)

Four years before his death, haiku master Matsuo Bashō looked back on his life and reflected upon the choices he had made. "I remember at one time I coveted an official post with a tenure of land," he remembered. Later he contemplated entering a monastery. "Yet I kept aimlessly wandering on like a cloud in the wind, all the while laboring to capture the beauty of flowers and birds." This, in the end, became his livelihood: poetry, the "thin line" to which Bashō clung because, he said, he lacked any other talent or ability.

To Bashō, the ideal poet carried a satchel on his back, wore straw sandals and a humble hat, and delighted in disciplining his mind through physical hardship so that he might attain "a knowledge of the true nature of things." It was this model Bashō sought to emulate throughout his life.

He did not set out to become a poet. He wrote his first haiku as a mere diversion while serving as a youngster in a feudal household near his birthplace outside Kyoto. Soon, however, Bashō developed a taste for the concise, 17-syllable form, and through the eloquence of his verse he eventually transformed haiku from a trifling pastime into a major literary genre.

Bashō devoted his life to writing. Even when he tired of poetry, and its accompanying fame, he found he could not renounce it. "I have tried to give up poetry and remain silent," he remarked toward the end of his life, "but every time I did so a poetic sentiment would solicit my heart and something would flicker in my mind. Such is the magic spell of poetry."

Much of Bashō's verse sprang from a sequence of long, mostly solitary journeys through Japan, which the poet undertook as a means of immersing himself in nature and thereby attaining spiritual serenity. In addition to poetry, Bashō's trips gave rise to a series of lyrical travel journals, most famously *The Narrow Road to the Deep North*, composed in 1689.

Even during the last year of his life Bashō continued to travel and write. In the fall of 1694 he contracted a stomach ailment from which he did not recover. On his deathbed he could think only of what he once called the "sinful attachment" of verse. Four days before his death Matsuo Bashō wrote his final poem:

> On a journey, ailing—
> My dreams roam about
> Over a withered moor.

Sunday

6

Daylight Saving Time begins

 Monday

7

William Wordsworth, b. 1770
Gabriela Mistral, b. 1889

Tuesday

8

Wednesday

9

Thursday

10

Clare Boothe Luce, b. 1903

Friday

11

Saturday

12

March						
S	M	T	W	T	F	S
						1
2	3	4	5	6	7	8
9	10	11	12	13	14	15
16	17	18	19	20	21	22
23	24	25	26	27	28	29
30	31					

April
1997

May						
S	M	T	W	T	F	S
					1	2	3
4	5	6	7	8	9	10
11	12	13	14	15	16	17
18	19	20	21	22	23	24
25	26	27	28	29	30	31

Sunday
13
Samuel Beckett, b. 1906   Nella Larsen, b. 1891

Monday
14

Tuesday
15

Henry James, b. 1843

Wednesday
16

Anatole France, b. 1844
J. M. Synge, b. 1871

Thursday
17

Isak Dinesen, b. 1885
Thornton Wilder, b. 1897

Friday
18

Saturday
19
Patriots' Day   *José Echegaray, b. 1832*

March						
S	M	T	W	T	F	S
						1
2	3	4	5	6	7	8
9	10	11	12	13	14	15
16	17	18	19	20	21	22
23	24	25	26	27	28	29
30	31					

April
1997

May						
S	M	T	W	T	F	S
					1	2	3
4	5	6	7	8	9	10
11	12	13	14	15	16	17
18	19	20	21	22	23	24
25	26	27	28	29	30	31

Nella Larsen
(April 13, 1891 - March 30, 1964)

Even for her time she was unorthodox. She smoked cigarettes, wore bobbed hair and short dresses, scorned religion, and used her maiden name for the publication of her books. Her greatest weakness, she said, was "dissatisfaction." Once, she confessed that although she was not quite sure what she wanted to be spiritually, "books, money, and travel would satisfy her materially."

Like the heroines of her novels, Nella Larsen was the product of a racially-mixed marriage, a fact that transformed her life as well as her work. The daughter of a white, Danish mother and a black, West Indian father, Larsen was comfortable in neither an all-white nor an all-black world. In the late 1920s, at the height of her success as a novelist, she admitted that she never saw her white mother or sister because "it might make it awkward for them."

Larsen began writing in 1925 while working as a children's librarian in the New York Public Library. She moved quickly from short stories to longer fiction, drafting her first novel, *Quicksand*, after five months of thinking about it and just six weeks at the typewriter. The book, a chronicle of the difficulties endured by a woman of racially-mixed ancestry, appeared in 1928 to enthusiastic reviews. A year later Larsen brought out a second novel, *Passing*, a work inspired in part by her readings of *Ulysses*. Like its predecessor, *Passing* dealt with the cultural conflict of mixed ancestry.

With *Passing*, Larsen's promise was confirmed. Silence followed. An unfounded charge of plagiarism, coupled with the deterioration of her marriage and the scandal of divorce, drove Larsen into seclusion. She tried but failed to complete a third, fourth, and fifth novel. At one point she concealed her whereabouts for two full years.

Born into the margins of American society, Larsen remained an outsider. She spent the last twenty years of her life working in obscurity as a nurse on Manhattan's Lower East Side. At her death in 1964, at age 72, few remembered Nella Larsen or what she had written. A biographer who tried in vain to find her obituary remarked that the author's exile had been so complete, "I couldn't even bury Nella Larsen."

It remained for a later generation to rekindle interest in this gifted recluse whose work and life reveal, writes critic Mary Helen Washington, that "behind the carefully manicured exterior, behind the appearance of security is a woman who hears the beating of her wings against a walled prison."

Ellen Glasgow
(April 22, 1873 - November 21, 1945)

"I was born a novelist," she said, "though I formed myself into an artist." A pioneer in the Southern Renaissance and in feminist writing, Glasgow broke free of the sentimental, romantic tradition to write honestly and skeptically about Southern society. "Tilling the fertile soil of man's vanity," she called it.

For most of her life she lived and worked in a spacious house at 1 West Main Street in Richmond, Virginia. She typed the first drafts of her novels in a large, second floor room surrounded by paintings of dogs, dog photographs, china dogs, and two large, frisky Sealyhams.

The ninth child in a family of ten children, she was so tiny and frail that for the first weeks of her life she was carried about on a pillow. Too weak to attend school regularly, Glasgow was tutored at home. She was strong enough, though, to rebel against her iron-willed father. "My mind is my own," she said. Writing novels seemed as natural to her as talking or walking. The heroine of her first novel, *The Descendant*, is an artist torn between work and love. "It is not fair!" she exclaims. "Why should men have everything in this world?" The book was rejected by one editor who told her to "stop writing, and go back to the South and have some babies." *Harper*'s bought it, and it was published anonymously. "When a bound copy of my first book reached me," Glasgow recalled, "I hid it under my pillow while a cousin, who had run in before breakfast, prattled beside my bed of the young men who had quarreled over the privilege of taking her to the ... Cotillion."

Glasgow was engaged twice, and had several love affairs, but she never married. Her many novels include *Barren Ground* (1925), *The Sheltered Life* (1932), and *In This Our Life* (1941), which won the Pulitzer Prize. She advised beginning writers to learn the technique of writing and then forget it. She had discovered that "ideas would not come to me if I went out to hunt for them ... but if I stopped and sank down into a kind of watchful reverie, they would flock back again like friendly pigeons."

In her fiction and particularly in her portrayal of women, Ellen Glasgow prepared the ground for a younger group of Southern writers, including William Faulkner, Thomas Wolfe, and Tennessee Williams. "The need of woman for woman was not written in the songs nor in the histories of men," she said, "but in the neglected and frustrated lives, which the songs and the histories of men had ignored."

Sunday
20

Monday
21

Charlotte Brontë, b. 1816
Passover begins at sunset

 Tuesday
22

Ellen Glasgow, b. 1873
Vladimir Nabokov, b. 1899
Madame de Staël, b. 1766

Wednesday
23

William Shakespeare, b. 1564
Bernard Malamud, b. 1914
Secretaries' Day

Thursday
24

Anthony Trollope, b. 1815

Friday
25

Anzac Day (N.Z.)
National Arbor Day

Saturday
26

March						
S	M	T	W	T	F	S
						1
2	3	4	5	6	7	8
9	10	11	12	13	14	15
16	17	18	19	20	21	22
23	24	25	26	27	28	29
30	31					

April
1997

May						
S	M	T	W	T	F	S
				1	2	3
4	5	6	7	8	9	10
11	12	13	14	15	16	17
18	19	20	21	22	23	24
25	26	27	28	29	30	31

Sunday
27
Mary Wollstonecraft, b. 1759   Edward Gibbon, b. 1737

Monday
28

Tuesday
29

Wednesday
30

Thursday
1

Friday
2

Saturday
3
Mikhail Bulgakov, b. 1891   William Inge, b. 1913   Niccolò Machiavelli, b. 1469

March						
S	M	T	W	T	F	S
						1
2	3	4	5	6	7	8
9	10	11	12	13	14	15
16	17	18	19	20	21	22
23	24	25	26	27	28	29
30	31					

April/May
1997

May						
S	M	T	W	T	F	S
				1	2	3
4	5	6	7	8	9	10
11	12	13	14	15	16	17
18	19	20	21	22	23	24
25	26	27	28	29	30	31

Edward Gibbon
(April 27, 1737—January 16, 1794)

Edward Gibbon was an ardent egotist.
"I was never less alone than when by myself,"
he reported.

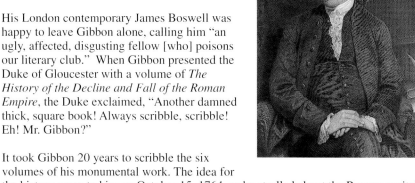

His London contemporary James Boswell was
happy to leave Gibbon alone, calling him "an
ugly, affected, disgusting fellow [who] poisons
our literary club." When Gibbon presented the
Duke of Gloucester with a volume of *The
History of the Decline and Fall of the Roman
Empire*, the Duke exclaimed, "Another damned
thick, square book! Always scribble, scribble!
Eh! Mr. Gibbon?"

It took Gibbon 20 years to scribble the six
volumes of his monumental work. The idea for
the history came to him on October 15, 1764, as he strolled about the Roman capital
listening to friars sing vespers. He felt as if he were in a dream, picturing the past
greatness of Rome and its people.

Twelve years later the first volume was published. His theme was "the triumph of
barbarism and Christianity," and because he treated the early Church and Christian
miracles with skepticism, sermons were preached against him and pamphlets accused
him of poor scholarship and even plagiarism.

Gibbon's careful scholarship, however, has withstood centuries. He composed his
sentences in his head before committing them to paper, writing elegantly and simply
in the balanced prose of the 18th century, as in this line about the Roman Comenus:
"In every deed of mischief he had a heart to resolve, a head to contrive, and a hand
to execute." In the next century, Samuel Coleridge would quip that "Gibbon's style
is detestable; but it is not the worst thing about him." Twentieth-century writer Frank
Sullivan complained that "just as the reader expected him to dish the dirt," Gibbon
would launch into a long Latin footnote to show off his own erudition and "to tease
readers who flunked Caesar."

Actually, Gibbon lacked a formal education. As a boy he had been too sickly to attend
school regularly, and he spent 14 "idle and unprofitable" months at Oxford. His aunt,
who had raised him after his mother died, instilled in him a love of reading which he
"would not exchange for the treasures of India." Writing his great work consumed his
life. He fell in love briefly with a young French woman, but he was not upset when his
father forbid the marriage. "I sighed as a lover, obeyed as a son," he said with
equanimity.

Disturbed by the "furious spirit of democracy" that swept the late-18th century, he
remained skeptical. "Corruption," he had opined in his Roman history, "[is] the most
infallible symptom of constitutional liberty."

James M. Barrie
(May 9, 1860 - June 21, 1937)

"Barrie has gone out of his mind," said British producer Herbert Beerbohm Tree after reading *Peter and Wendy.* The script called for a huge cast, including a dog nurse, an alligator who swallowed an alarm clock, a fairy named Tinker Bell, and a terrifying pirate with a hook for a hand. Tree turned down the play. James Barrie sent it to American producer Charles Frohman, who loved it and suggested that Barrie call it *Peter Pan.*

Barrie dedicated *Peter Pan* to the five sons of Arthur and Sylvia Davies. "I suppose I always knew that I made Peter by rubbing the five of you violently together, as savages with two sticks produce a flame," Barrie said. His friendship with the Davies' boys sparked his creativity, but the source of the play can be found in his childhood.

When James Barrie was six, his 13-year old brother David was killed in a skating accident. To comfort his grieving mother, James wore his brother's clothes, imitated his whistle, and his wide-legged stance, but he could not replace his dead brother in his mother's affections. David would always be the boy who never grew up. And, James, who would never grow past five feet tall, would also be the boy who could never grow up.

Shy and insecure about his diminutive size, Barrie created alternative selves. In his early days as a journalist in Scotland, Barrie would dash off articles by pretending to be various characters, such as a doctor, a blacksmith, a policeman, or a bishop. He prided himself on being able to write about anything. Challenged to write about a scrap of paper that had been blown into the gutter, he "found it quite easy. The editor took it, too!"

Barrie's first novel, *The Little Minister*, established his reputation. During his unhappy marriage to actress Mary Ansell (who later divorced him), Barrie enjoyed success as a playwright, writing *The Admirable Crichton*, *Dear Brutus*, *What Every Woman Knows*, and, of course, *Peter Pan.* Barrie's literary friends included Thomas Hardy, George Bernard Shaw, and H. G. Wells, who all towered over him. He likened his own talent to kicking up pebbles, attributing his success to luck and "farce, invention, contrivance, and industry."

If he had only grown to be "six feet three inches," Barrie said, "it would have made a great difference in my life. I would not have bothered turning out reels of printed matter. My one aim would have been to become a favourite of the ladies ... The things I could have said to them if my legs had been longer."

Sunday
4

Monday
5

May Day Holiday (U.K.)

 Tuesday
6

Sigmund Freud, b. 1856

Wednesday
7

Rabindranath Tagore, b. 1861
Edward Lear, b. 1812

Thursday
8

Muharram, Islamic Year 1418 A.H.

Friday
9

James M. Barrie, b. 1860

Saturday
10

Benito Pérez Galdós, b. 1843

April						
S	M	T	W	T	F	S
		1	2	3	4	5
6	7	8	9	10	11	12
13	14	15	16	17	18	19
20	21	22	23	24	25	26
27	28	29	30			

May
1997

June						
S	M	T	W	T	F	S
1	2	3	4	5	6	7
8	9	10	11	12	13	14
15	16	17	18	19	20	21
22	23	24	25	26	27	28
29	30					

Sunday

11

Mothers' Day   *Mari Sandoz, b. 1896*

Monday

12

Daphne du Maurier, b. 1907

Tuesday

13

Wednesday

14

Dante Alighieri, b. 1265

Thursday

15

Katharine Anne Porter, b. 1890
L. Frank Baum, b. 1856

Friday

16

Saturday

17

Armed Forces Day   *Dorothy Richardson, b. 1873*

April						
S	M	T	W	T	F	S
		1	2	3	4	5
6	7	8	9	10	11	12
13	14	15	16	17	18	19
20	21	22	23	24	25	26
27	28	29	30			

May
1997

June						
S	M	T	W	T	F	S
1	2	3	4	5	6	7
8	9	10	11	12	13	14
15	16	17	18	19	20	21
22	23	24	25	26	27	28
29	30					

Dorothy Richardson
(May 17, 1873 - June 17, 1957)

Most readers believed Dorothy Richardson's multivolume novel *Pilgrimage* was pure fiction. Few knew the huge work traced Richardson's own life between the ages of 17 and 40, recounting, volume by volume, her feelings as an adolescent, her passage into adulthood, her fleeting career as a dentist's secretary, her mother's suicide, her abiding love of London.

Few knew that Richardson's work was autobiographical because, paradoxically, Richardson herself was an intensely private person. She did not grant an interview until 1931—16 years after the publication of the first volume of *Pilgrimage*. Photographs of her were so rare that *The New York Times Book Review* accidentally printed a wrong likeness of Richardson to accompany a 1927 review of one of her books.

She learned her craft from her friend and sometime lover, H. G. Wells, who was the first writer she ever met. Wells taught Richardson to regard the day-to-day routines of her life—her work in the dentist's office, lunch in a cheap restaurant—as fodder for narrative. When he responded with admiration to her written descriptions of everyday events, praising her sharp eye and instinct for structure, Richardson began to sense she had potential as a writer.

At 40 she started work on *Pilgrimage*, and she devoted most of the rest of her life to its composition. In the work, which eventually numbered 13 volumes, she mythologized her life, giving aesthetic shape to the events and passions she had experienced as a woman.

The book eluded her at first. But after a frustrating series of false starts, Richardson found the solitude and focus she needed in order to chart her path. The result was an experimental prose style in which Richardson endeavored to capture consciousness in its flow.

Virginia Woolf, one of the novel's many admirers, observed that in *Pilgrimage* Richardson invented a new kind of sentence with a distinctly "feminine gender. It is of a more elastic fiber than the old, capable of stretching to the extreme, of suspending the frailest particles, of enveloping the vaguest shapes." Novelist May Sinclair was more succinct. Borrowing from William James, Sinclair described Richardson's prose style as "stream of consciousness."

Richardson herself eschewed labels. With her artist husband she lived a frugal life, dividing her time between London and Cornwall. In her last years she abandoned fiction and spent her time, instead, writing letters to friends and relatives. She remained intent to the end on finding the most direct means of expressing herself and her ideas.

Arthur Conan Doyle
(May 22, 1859 - July 7, 1930)

As a boy, Arthur Conan Doyle read
so voraciously and so rapidly that the
Edinburgh library informed his mother
he would not be allowed to check out
books more than twice a day. Not
satisfied with reading adventure stories,
he tried writing one of his own—a story
about a man and a tiger. He complained
"that it was easy to get people into
scrapes, but not so easy to get them
out again."

At boarding school in England, he
practiced his narrative skills by telling
his classmates bloodcurdling tales of
mystery and suspense. When he was 17,
he entered Edinburgh University to study
medicine. There he served as outpatient
clerk to Dr. Joseph Bell, an eagle-eyed
surgeon with unusual diagnostic skills
and an "eerie trick of spotting details."

For nine years, from 1881 to 1890, Doyle practiced medicine. His financial
pressures increased after his marriage, and he sold short stories at about $4 apiece to
supplement his income. The stories weren't very good. "It is a great mistake," he said,
"to start putting out cargo when you have hardly stowed any on board."

Edgar Allen Poe, who had created the great detective M. Dupin, inspired him to invent
a detective of his own and to give him the deductive reasoning skills possessed by Dr.
Bell, Doyle's old teacher. But what to call him? Sherringford Holmes didn't have the
right ring; finally, Doyle decided on Sherlock Holmes. To narrate the exploits of the
modest Holmes, Doyle looked in the mirror and created Dr. Watson, a character
modeled after himself.

In writing, "the first thing is to get your idea," Doyle advised. Before he began a book,
he knew the entire story from beginning to end. He admitted that in ordinary life he
was not observant and had "to throw myself into an artificial frame of mind" to write.

In 1902, Doyle was knighted at Buckingham Palace. He wrote and lectured around the
world until a year before his death. He is buried in the rose garden of his home under
an oak headstone that reads "Steel True, Blade Straight."

Even though his creator died, Sherlock Holmes continues to leap from the pages of
Doyle's books into movies, theater, and television. He lives, too, in our imagination,
puffing on his pipe, staring at us with those penetrating eyes. "You see, but you do
not observe," he tells us.

Sunday
18

Monday
19

Lorraine Hansberry, b. 1930
Victoria Day (Canada)

Tuesday
20

Honoré Balzac, b. 1799

Wednesday
21

Thursday
22

Arthur Conan Doyle, b. 1859

Friday
23

Saturday
24

April						
S	M	T	W	T	F	S
		1	2	3	4	5
6	7	8	9	10	11	12
13	14	15	16	17	18	19
20	21	22	23	24	25	26
27	28	29	30			

May
1997

June						
S	M	T	W	T	F	S
1	2	3	4	5	6	7
8	9	10	11	12	13	14
15	16	17	18	19	20	21
22	23	24	25	26	27	28
29	30					

Sunday
25

Ralph Waldo Emerson, b. 1803   Raymond Carver, b. 1938   Theodore Roethke, b. 1908

Monday
26

Memorial Day
Spring Holiday (U.K. ex. Scotland)

Tuesday
27

Rachel Carson, b. 1907
Dashiell Hammett, b. 1894
John Cheever, b. 1912

Wednesday
28

Patrick White, b. 1912

Thursday
29

Friday
30

Saturday
31
Walt Whitman, b. 1819

| April |
S M T W T F S
1 2 3 4 5
6 7 8 9 10 11 12
13 14 15 16 17 18 19
20 21 22 23 24 25 26
27 28 29 30

May
1997

| June |
S M T W T F S
1 2 3 4 5 6 7
8 9 10 11 12 13 14
15 16 17 18 19 20 21
22 23 24 25 26 27 28
29 30

Theodore Roethke
(May 25, 1908 - August 1, 1963)

Poetry, wrote Theodore Roethke, is "shot
through with appeals to the unconscious, to
the fears and desires that go far back into our
childhood, into the imagination of the race."

In his own work Roethke dug through the
sediment of his past: the greenhouse his
German-immigrant father owned and worked
in central Michigan, the field beyond the
greenhouse where Roethke played as a child,
the pickle factory where he worked as an
undergraduate, his father's death during
Roethke's adolescence—an event to which
the poet returned imaginatively time and
again throughout his life.

In college Theodore Roethke swaggered about campus in a coonskin coat. He stood
over 6' tall and weighed 190 pounds. A tennis player and fraternity man, he cultivated
an image of himself as a tough guy with underworld connections. In truth he was an
introspective literature student who harbored a secret ambition to write poetry. As an
adult he drank heavily, drifted in and out of teaching jobs, and suffered repeated
mental breakdowns that sent him periodically into the hospital and in 1945 led to a
series of shock treatments.

Through it all Roethke wrote. Blessed with a rare imagination and an extraordinary
command of the techniques of prosody, he was, in the words of critic Harvey Gross,
"one of our modern masters of meter and rhythm." With his first book, *Open House*
(1941), Roethke earned good reviews from the likes of W. H. Auden and Louise
Bogan. But it was his second book, *The Lost Son* (1948), with its acutely original
passages on plant and animal life, and its author's long meditation on his father's
death in the title poem, that made Roethke's name.

Theodore Roethke believed that one of the poet's "supreme duties" was "to question
and to affirm," and he devoted much of his life to that end. Wherever he went he
carried a notebook with him in order to jot down lines and images as they occurred to
him. From these jottings he constructed his poems. At his death in 1963, at 55, he left
behind 227 such notebooks.

In one of his final poems, "Once More, the Round," Roethke wrote rapturously of life:

> And I dance with William Blake
> For love, for Love's sake;
>
> And everything comes to One,
> As we dance on, dance on, dance on.

Sappho
(600 B.C. - ?)

Plato called her the tenth muse. Solon of Athens wished to learn a poem of Sappho's and then die. She influenced poets who came after her, including Tennyson, Pope, Swinburne, Hardy, and Pound, who wrote poetry in "Sapphic meter." Sara Teasdale praised her as the "sole perfect singer that the world has heard."

Little is known of Sappho's life. She was born in the 6th century B.C. on the isle of Lesbos into an aristocratic family. The term "lesbian" is derived from the name of her island home. Like Socrates, who gathered a group of young male followers, Sappho led and taught a circle of young women. She may have married and had a daughter.

From her poetry, which is often addressed to specific women in her circle, we know that she loved women passionately. The ancients were able to read her classic love poetry in nine books, but only fragments have survived. Many of her lines were quoted in journals, letters, and papers of later writers.

Reading Sappho's incomplete verses is like "hearing faint snatches of a human voice, coming up through a vast chasm of deep silence," observed one Sappho scholar. "Now I shall sing these delightful songs, beautifully, to my girls," Sappho writes.

Her songs express her feelings with an immediacy that seems completely modern. "I don't know what to do," she says. "I am of two minds." About love, she seems certain. It is "the most beautiful thing on the dark earth." Sometimes love fails, and she sings of loss. She lies alone "in the deep middle of the night," but her song seems to call love forth. Few poets have written so urgently and so beautifully about physical passion:

> Desire shakes me once again;
> here is that melting of my limbs.
> It is a creeping thing, and bittersweet.
> I can do nothing to resist.

Sunday
1

Monday
2

Thomas Hardy, b. 1840
Queen's Birthday (N.Z.)
Holiday (Rep. of Ireland)

Tuesday
3

Wednesday
4

 Thursday
5

Federico García Lorca, b. 1898

Friday
6

Saturday
7

May
S M T W T F S
1 2 3
4 5 6 7 8 9 10
11 12 13 14 15 16 17
18 19 20 21 22 23 24
25 26 27 28 29 30 31

June
1997

July
S M T W T F S
1 2 3 4 5
6 7 8 9 10 11 12
13 14 15 16 17 18 19
20 21 22 23 24 25 26
27 28 29 30 31

Sunday
8
Marguerite Yourcenar, b. 1903

Monday
9

Tuesday
10

Wednesday
11

Ben Jonson, b. 1572

Thursday
12

Anne Frank, b. 1929
Djuna Barnes, b. 1892

Friday
13

Fanny Burney, b. 1752
William Butler Yeats, b. 1865

Saturday
14
Flag Day   *Harriet Beecher Stowe, b. 1811*

		May				
S	M	T	W	T	F	S
				1	2	3
4	5	6	7	8	9	10
11	12	13	14	15	16	17
18	19	20	21	22	23	24
25	26	27	28	29	30	31

June
1997

		July				
S	M	T	W	T	F	S
		1	2	3	4	5
6	7	8	9	10	11	12
13	14	15	16	17	18	19
20	21	22	23	24	25	26
27	28	29	30	31		

Ben Jonson
(June 11, 1572 - August 6, 1637)

He hated Johnson, his commonplace name,
so he became Jonson. While Shakespeare,
his contemporary with the more elegant name,
attended a free grammar school in Stratford,
Jonson, who lived in a tenement in
Westminster, depended on a family friend
who paid his way to Westminster School.
From 7 a.m. to 6 p.m. Latin grammar was
literally beaten into him. Luckily, he studied
with William Camden, a brilliant teacher,
who introduced him to the literature of
classical Greece and Rome and taught him
to love poetry.

Because of his poverty, Jonson didn't continue his education at Oxford or Cambridge.
Instead, he became a bricklayer like his stepfather. Legend says that he worked with a
trowel in one hand and a book in the other. His memory was prodigious, and he
bragged, "I can repeat whole books that I have read."

After years of toiling as a bricklayer, Jonson worked as an actor in a strolling company
before moving to London. The flourishing theatre world on the outskirts of the city
offered an exciting life based on merit rather than social status. In Jonson's first
important play, *Every Man in His Humour*, William Shakespeare, then 34 and the
author of more than a dozen plays, acted a comic part.

Jonson's career almost came to an abrupt end when he fought a duel with an actor.
Convicted of murdering the actor, Jonson escaped execution through a loophole in the
law. To prevent him from using the loophole again, Jonson was branded on the thumb
with the letter "T."

A favorite of James I, for 20 years Jonson wrote beautiful court masques designed
by Inigo Jones. He is remembered, though, for his popular comedies, particularly
Volpone, *The Alchemist*, and *Bartholomew Fair*.

Jonson loved "gentle Shakespeare," but he disapproved of his rival's improbable
plots and fanciful settings. At the Mermaid Tavern over tankards of Canary wine, he
championed his own satirical, realistic art with his loyal followers, called "Sons of
Ben." Unlike Shakespeare, who—according to the players—never blotted a line,
Jonson revised carefully. Jonson was "a huge galleon," recalled one witness, "solid
but slow in his performances" while Shakespeare was the "English man-of-war
who took advantage of all winds by the quickness of his wit and invention."

At his death, Ben Jonson's estate amounted to a wicker chair and eight pounds, eight
shillings and ten-pence. His art, though, earned him a place in Westminster Abbey—
where his marble marker reads "O Rare Ben Jonson."

Philip Barry
(June 18, 1896 - December 3, 1949)

Broadway memoirs are filled with countless anecdotes about Philip Barry's more colorful contemporaries, like George S. Kaufman, Ben Hecht, and Charles MacArthur. Barry, an urbane Anglophile, remained aloof from show business and retreated to the world of the rich in Philadelphia, Hobe Sound, and Cannes.

Educated at Yale and a member of George Pierce Baker's famed Workshop 47 at Harvard, Barry achieved Broadway success with *You and I* in 1923. The play ran for 170 performances and earned him $700 a week. Two years later, *In A Garden*, starring the gifted Laurette Taylor, was a flop. At the close of the final performance, Taylor enraged Barry by telling the audience, "Perhaps our playwright isn't ready yet. Perhaps we did a disservice to his brilliant talent by producing him too soon."

Barry kept writing, penning 22 plays in all, including *Paris Bound*, *Holiday*, *Hotel Universe*, and *The Animal Kingdom*. He wrote about the comfortable, jaded lives of the wealthy with sophisticated, satiric accuracy. Born into the middle class, Barry moved into the upper class when he married debutante Ellen Semple. One of their wedding presents was a villa on the French Riviera where they hobnobbed with Scott and Zelda Fitzgerald, Gerald and Sara Murphy, and Ernest Hemingway.

His comedies were popular, but critics and audiences rejected his darker dramas, which often contained moral messages. "If you have a message send for Western Union," George S. Kaufman advised. In 1939, Barry returned to his high comic style with *The Philadelphia Story*, starring Katharine Hepburn as Tracy Lord. Barry modeled the character after Hope Scott, the reigning queen of Philadelphia society. Barry was friendly with Hope and her husband, Edgar, who lived on Philadelphia's Main Line. He visited them at Androssan, their 50-room Georgian brick mansion with 13-foot ceilings and a dining table that seated 32 for dinner. Barry dedicated the play to Hope, who "liked to say shocking things in her perfect lockjaw brogue and then wait for the reaction."

While *The Philadelphia Story* is revived often, and the movie has become a classic, Barry's other plays remain largely unproduced today. Few American playwrights, though, wrote more knowingly about the arrogance and self-absorption of the rich.

In *Paris Bound*, an adulterous husband reconciles with his wife. "You haven't forgotten anything," the husband says in the last scene. "Not a thing. Just my dignity," answers his wife. "That's not serious," replies the husband.

Sunday
15
Fathers' Day

Monday
16

Tuesday
17

John Hersey, b. 1914
Wednesday
18

Philip Barry, b. 1896
Thursday
19

Blaise Pascal, b. 1623
 Friday
20

Lillian Hellman, b. 1905
Saturday
21
Mary McCarthy, b. 1912   Summer Solstice, 4:21 am EDT

May						
S	M	T	W	T	F	S
				1	2	3
4	5	6	7	8	9	10
11	12	13	14	15	16	17
18	19	20	21	22	23	24
25	26	27	28	29	30	31

June
1997

July						
S	M	T	W	T	F	S
		1	2	3	4	5
6	7	8	9	10	11	12
13	14	15	16	17	18	19
20	21	22	23	24	25	26
27	28	29	30	31		

Sunday
22
Erich Maria Remarque, b. 1898

Monday
23

Anna Akhmatova, b. 1889

Tuesday
24

St. John of the Cross, b. 1542

Wednesday
25

Thursday
26

Pearl Buck, b. 1892

Friday
27

Helen Keller, b. 1880

Saturday
28
Luigi Pirandello, b. 1867

May						
S	M	T	W	T	F	S
					1	2	3
4	5	6	7	8	9	10
11	12	13	14	15	16	17
18	19	20	21	22	23	24
25	26	27	28	29	30	31

June
1997

July						
S	M	T	W	T	F	S
		1	2	3	4	5
6	7	8	9	10	11	12
13	14	15	16	17	18	19
20	21	22	23	24	25	26
27	28	29	30	31		

Anna Akhmatova
(June 23, 1889 - March 5, 1966)

She has been called an "icon of suffering and
authenticity," a "goddess of mourning," and,
in the memorable words of her disciple Joseph
Brodsky, "the keening muse."

She knew unspeakable pain. She withstood
the Russian Revolution, the Nazi siege of
Leningrad, and Stalin's terror. Her first husband
was executed by firing squad in 1921; her third
husband died in a Siberian prison camp in 1953.
She was with her friend Osip Mandelstam when
he was arrested; later, like most of her friends,
Mandelstam died in Stalin's camps.

When her son, Lev, was arrested during
the worst years of the purges, between 1935
and 1940, Anna Akhmatova stood outside
Leningrad's huge stone prison daily for 17 months, one of an endless line of women
desperate for some word of their loved ones. Akhmatova was by then a famous poet.
One day a woman recognized her. "Can you describe this?" the woman asked.

"I can," said Akhmatova. Born of this exchange, her poem cycle *Requiem*, in which
she recounted the agony of a mother trying to discover her son's fate, went on to
become a popular epic, passed on by mouth from one generation to the next.

In 1946 Akhmatova was expelled from the Union of Soviet Writers. Her apartment in
Leningrad was bugged. The K.G.B. forced the domestic help to report on her activities
and friends. During these years Akhmatova lived in a single room with a small bed, a
tiny desk, and four books—Pushkin, Shakespeare, Dante, and the Bible—which she
kept hidden from pilfering neighbors. She did most of her writing while sitting on a
window ledge.

Because her work was banned from publication, Akhmatova regularly burned her
manuscripts. "It was like a ritual," a friend remembered. "Hands, matches, an ashtray.
A ritual beautiful and bitter." While her poems burned, Akhmatova sat and talked
about the weather.

Trusted friends committed her poetry to memory in order to preserve it, and
Akhmatova's fame endured. Despite the deprivations of her life, she never lost her
gift for candor. Described by friends as both madcap and beautiful, she once said of
herself that she was "written by Kafka and acted by Chaplin."

In her poem "The Return," Akhmatova observed that the souls of all those she loved
had "flown to the stars. Thank God there's no one left for me to lose so I can cry."

Antoine de Saint-Exupéry
(June 29, 1900 - July 31, 1944)

Sometimes, while flying the weekly mail route between Buenos Aires and Patagonia, aviator Antoine de Saint-Exupéry faced windstorms so fierce he was unable to reach the coast just 600 feet away. A 900-foot climb could take him over an hour to complete. Even under the best of conditions, he needed the help of a dozen Argentine soldiers in order to land. As Saint-Exupéry approached the earth, the soldiers would run alongside his plane with long bamboo poles, which they hooked into the underside of his wings so that despite the winds both the pilot and his aircraft were secure.

This was in 1930. Five years later, while attempting to break the time record for flight between Paris and Saigon, Saint-Ex (as he was to become known) and his mechanic crashed in the Sahara and wandered for five days before they were found by Bedouins. Close to death from dehydration, Saint-Ex survived to write movingly of the ordeal and of the nomad who first spotted him.

Literature and flight. He fell in love with both as a young man and devoted his life to their achievement. "One must not learn to write but to see," he told a friend in 1923. In his books—among them *Night Flight*; *Wind, Sand and Stars*; *Flight to Arras*— Antoine de Saint-Exupéry did just that, describing things as they would appear to a plane flying at low altitude: a grove of orange trees, a stream, a group of fishermen on the beach.

Tall and gangling, Saint-Exupéry never fit comfortably into either of the two worlds he revered. His fellow pilots thought him strange because of his fondness for literature and the literary life. Writers in Parisian cafés, where he spent much of his time, found him odd because of his passion for something so dangerous as flight.

At the outbreak of World War II, Saint-Ex left France for New York City. Although he disliked North America, he wrote his best known work there, *The Little Prince*, the fanciful story of a small traveler from a distant asteroid.

In 1943, Saint-Exupéry left New York to join the Free French forces in North Africa. Despite his age—43—he was cleared to fly high-altitude reconnaissance missions. On what was to have been his last flight, over German-occupied southern France, both Saint-Exupéry and his plane disappeared. No trace of either has ever been found.

Sunday

29

Antoine de Saint-Exupéry, b. 1900

Monday

30

Tuesday

1

George Sand, b. 1804
Susan Glaspell, b. 1873
Canada Day

Wednesday

2

Thursday

3

Franz Kafka, b. 1883

 Friday

4

Nathaniel Hawthorne, b. 1804
Declaration of Independence, 1776

Saturday

5

Jean Cocteau, b. 1889

			May			
S	M	T	W	T	F	S
				1	2	3
4	5	6	7	8	9	10
11	12	13	14	15	16	17
18	19	20	21	22	23	24
25	26	27	28	29	30	31

June/July
1997

			July			
S	M	T	W	T	F	S
		1	2	3	4	5
6	7	8	9	10	11	12
13	14	15	16	17	18	19
20	21	22	23	24	25	26
27	28	29	30	31		

Sunday
6

Monday
7

Tuesday
8

Wednesday
9

Thursday
10

Friday
11

Saturday
12

June						
S	M	T	W	T	F	S
1	2	3	4	5	6	7
8	9	10	11	12	13	14
15	16	17	18	19	20	21
22	23	24	25	26	27	28
29	30					

July
1997

August						
S	M	T	W	T	F	S
					1	2
3	4	5	6	7	8	9
10	11	12	13	14	15	16
17	18	19	20	21	22	23
24	25	26	27	28	29	30
31						

Johanna Spyri
(July 12, 1827 - July 7, 1901)

In the old Swiss farmhouse that served as a village school, young Johanna Spyri struggled to get through the days. She disliked studying and hated the classroom. When she tried to make a drawing, she spent more time erasing than sketching. One day she rubbed a hole so big in her drawing paper that she laughed out loud. "Hannili, you will be a dunce!" warned the school's old, snuff-taking teacher, Herr Strickler.

At home it was a different story. Every Sunday night Johanna's father required each of his eight children to turn in a bit of original verse. Johanna not only wrote her weekly poem with ease, she turned in verse for her younger brothers and sisters as well. She also wrote charades for her family to perform.

Plate from a 1915 edition of *Heidi* illustrated by Maria Kirk

But Spyri waited until she was 43 years old to begin writing professionally. She wrote her first stories in 1870, in an attempt to raise money for the refugees of the Franco-Prussian War who came streaming across the border into her native Zurich. Her stories sold so well that Spyri ventured to try her hand at a longer work. The result was her first full-length book, *Heidi*.

The story of a Swiss orphan and her bucolic life in the Alps, *Heidi* was published in 1880 and to Spyri's amazement became an instant bestseller. Within ten years the book went through thirteen German editions; it made its American debut in 1899. Shirley Temple starred in the first film adaptation of *Heidi* in 1937. Sixty years later, *Heidi* continues to enchant young people across the world—many of whom pay unwitting tribute to the book by naming their pets and dolls after its heroine.

For *Heidi*'s bashful author, the book's success meant a sudden and unwelcome interest in her private life. Johanna Spyri insisted, however, that it was not she who mattered but her books. A modest housewife with a placid face and a thick, coronet braid, Spyri continued living and writing in Zurich as she had always done, despite her international fame.

Four years after *Heidi*'s publication, Spyri's husband, Bernhard, died. Her only son succumbed to tuberculosis while he was still a student. Spyri endured these losses by devoting herself to writing. She completed at least 50 children's stories before her own death in 1901. Throughout her work Spyri celebrates the lush beauty of Switzerland. The woman who once struggled to fill her schoolgirl sketchbooks ultimately gave the world an enduring portrait of her homeland.

The French Revolution

When the citizens of Paris stormed the Bastille on July 14, 1789, they unleashed a revolution of words as well as politics. Language— drawn as much from classical Greek and Roman oratory as from the writings of Jean-Jacques Rousseau and Immanuel Kant—became a deadly weapon in that

Taking the Bastille, July 14, 1789

bloody insurrection, and language continues to be one of the ways by which we know it best.

The men who led the revolution—Robespierre, Danton, Desmoulins, and their Jacobin colleagues—were powerful orators who seized control of the government largely through their ability to give speeches. Even when the tide turned, and they became the victims of their own revolt, they went on giving speeches—in courtrooms, in prison, on their way to the guillotine.

The revolution changed the French language. The word "citizen" replaced the word "monsieur"; the "French nation" became the "the people." A popular song by Rouget de Lisle, *La Marseillaise*, rallied the citizens of France with its revolutionary cry: "Marchons! Marchons!"

At home and abroad, writers responded passionately to the explosive news from Paris. William Wordsworth spent most of the year 1792 in France. He witnessed the massacre of more than a thousand prisoners in Paris, visited the sights where atrocities had occurred, and recorded his horror at it all in his long poem *The Prelude*.

Soon after the storming of the Bastille, William Blake also turned to verse in an attempt to shape his response to the revolution. In Germany, Schiller and Kleist each wrote about the rebellion; in England, Jane Austen copied out the *Marseillaise*, and Mary Wollstonecraft published her thoughts on the *Origin and Progress of the French Revolution and the Effect It Has Produced in Europe*.

Within decades of the event, historians Edmund Burke, Thomas Carlyle, Alexis de Tocqueville, and Jules Michelet had all published accounts of the revolution. Their work became an indispensable resource not only for future historians but also for playwrights, novelists, and poets who later turned to the French Revolution as inspiration—among them Balzac, Hugo, Büchner, Lamartine, Chateaubriand, Dickens, and in our own century Alejo Carpentier and Peter Weiss.

But of the thousands of books, poems, and memoirs to emerge from the French Revolution, none is perhaps more moving than the letter Marie Antoinette wrote to her sister from prison on the eve of her execution. "Farewell my good and kind sister," she wrote. "May this letter reach you. I embrace you with all my heart, together with my poor, dear children. My God it breaks my heart to leave them forever. Farewell, farewell ..." Her letter was never delivered.

Sunday
13

Monday
14

F. R. Leavis, b. 1895
Isaac Bashevis Singer, b. 1904
Holiday (N. Ireland)

Tuesday
15

Wednesday
16

Thursday
17

Mawlid, Prophet Mohammed born c. 570

Friday
18

William Makepeace Thackeray, b. 1811

 Saturday
19

	June					
S	**M**	**T**	**W**	**T**	**F**	**S**
1	2	3	4	5	6	7
8	9	10	11	12	13	14
15	16	17	18	19	20	21
22	23	24	25	26	27	28
29	30					

July
1997

	August					
S	**M**	**T**	**W**	**T**	**F**	**S**
					1	2
3	4	5	6	7	8	9
10	11	12	13	14	15	16
17	18	19	20	21	22	23
24	25	26	27	28	29	30
31						

Sunday
20

Petrarch, b. 1304

Monday
21

Hart Crane, b. 1899
John Gardner, b. 1933
Ernest Hemingway, b. 1899

Tuesday
22

Wednesday
23

Thursday
24

Alexandre Dumas, père, b. 1802

Friday
25

Saturday
26

George Bernard Shaw, b. 1856   Antonio Machado, b. 1875

		June				
S	M	T	W	T	F	S
1	2	3	4	5	6	7
8	9	10	11	12	13	14
15	16	17	18	19	20	21
22	23	24	25	26	27	28
29	30					

July
1997

		August				
S	M	T	W	T	F	S
					1	2
3	4	5	6	7	8	9
10	11	12	13	14	15	16
17	18	19	20	21	22	23
24	25	26	27	28	29	30
31						

Antonio Machado
(July 26, 1875 - February 22, 1939)

In his bowler hat and shabby black suit with
cigarette ashes scattered across its lapels,
Antonio Machado cut a mournful figure. He
was a solitary man who titled his first poetry
collection *Solitudes*. In it he wrote of time,
memory, and the enchanted world of his
childhood in southern Spain—the orange
and lemon trees that filled the patio of his
home in Seville, the sound of children's
voices spilling from a plaza nearby.

He was in his early 30s when he took his first
job, teaching high-school French in the town
of Soria in northern Spain. The work was
dull. But Machado fell in love with the
beautiful young daughter of his landlady, and
in 1909 they married. He was 35 at the time
of his wedding; his bride, Leonor, was 16.

For a brief time Machado was blissfully content. Then Leonor suddenly contracted
tuberculosis. She died in 1912, and Machado, reeling with grief, left Soria for another
teaching post in the tiny southern town of Baeza, where he would not be reminded of
his young wife.

Of Baeza, Machado observed: "There is only one bookstore, where they sell post-
cards, prayer books, and magazines, both clerical and pornographic." He taught
French in the little town and struggled to quell his sorrow. Neighbors grew accus-
tomed to the sight of him roaming the streets alone like a vagrant. Sometimes he
wandered 15 miles of twisting road to a nearby town for a cup of coffee, then
returned, on foot, to Baeza. Occasionally he managed to write poems.

Machado described the poet as "a poor creature in a dream, / groping for God
perpetually in the mist." He defined poetry as "an anvil of constant spiritual activity. ...
All our efforts," he said, "ought to reach out toward light, toward consciousness."

In his works—especially *Solitudes* (1903) and *The Castilian Country* (1912)—
Machado memorialized both the Spanish landscape and his own, inner landscape,
writing with a simplicity of language that has since inspired generations of poets,
both in Spain and abroad.

In 1939, during the last months of the Spanish Civil War, Machado fled Spain for
France. En route to Paris he caught pneumonia and fell gravely ill. His last request
was that he be buried in Spanish earth. By night, a group of his fellow refugees
slipped across the border and dug up sackfuls of Spanish soil, which they brought
back to France in time for Machado's funeral. They packed it around his coffin, so
that in the end his wish was fulfilled.

Booth Tarkington
(July 29, 1869 - May 19, 1946)

He's largely forgotten now, but
for a time, Booth Tarkington was
called the "Dean of American
Letters." He sought to make his
readers feel "full of courage and
the capacity for happiness in a
brightened world." Critics charged
him with "neglecting the consequen-
tial, evading the provocative, and
avoiding the controversial."

Tarkington had little firsthand knowledge of anything provocative or controversial.
Born and raised in Indianapolis, he enjoyed an idyllic childhood. His lawyer father
and his refined mother read aloud to him daily from Shakespeare, Dickens, Victor
Hugo, and French history. On his own, he read dime thrillers, and his first finished
play was a 14-act melodrama about Jesse James.

After attending Phillips Exeter Academy and Princeton, Tarkington returned to the
family home in Indianapolis to become a writer. For six years, supported by his
parents and a legacy from a rich uncle, he wrote and was rejected, earning a total
of $22.50.

His first break came when Hamlin Garland at *McClure's* magazine read his novel
The Man from Indiana. "You are a novelist," Garland told him. The book was a
bestseller. In 1913, with the publication of *Penrod*, followed by *Seventeen* in 1915,
Tarkington became a popular juvenile author. In his adult fiction, Tarkington aimed
at the middlebrows, who shared his own values of optimism and faith in the American
way. Tarkington wrote clearly and humorously, feeling that comedy is "the third best
thing in life." He published about three-dozen novels, some two-dozen plays, many
short stories and articles, and won the Pulitzer Prize twice, for his novels *Alice
Adams* and *The Magnificent Ambersons*.

A millionaire writer who was rejected by the critics, Tarkington was bourgeois in a
bohemian literary world. "There is not a thing you cannot talk about in a novel," he
asserted, "if you have good manners and know how to talk about it without dragging
in the livery stable and the dissecting room." At a time when James Joyce and D. H.
Lawrence were writing explicitly about sex, Tarkington countered that in writing love
scenes, "if a person stood in a pouring rain for an hour, there is no need to say that he
got wet."

Tarkington's dedication to his work sustained him during his darkest hours. As his
only child lay dying, he said, "I must work: I must go on with this novel. If I
shouldn't, I'd be wrecked, I think."

Sunday
27

Monday
28

Beatrix Potter, b. 1866
Gerard Manley Hopkins, b. 1844

Tuesday
29

Booth Tarkington, b. 1869

Wednesday
30

Giorgio Vasari, b. 1511
Emily Brontë, b. 1818

Thursday
31

Friday
1

Herman Melville, b. 1819

Saturday
2

James Baldwin, b. 1924

June						
S	M	T	W	T	F	S
1	2	3	4	5	6	7
8	9	10	11	12	13	14
15	16	17	18	19	20	21
22	23	24	25	26	27	28
29	30					

July/August
1997

August						
S	M	T	W	T	F	S
					1	2
3	4	5	6	7	8	9
10	11	12	13	14	15	16
17	18	19	20	21	22	23
24	25	26	27	28	29	30
31						

Sunday
3

Monday
4

Knut Hamsun, b. 1859
Holiday (Rep. of Ireland)

Tuesday
5

Wednesday
6

Alfred Lord Tennyson, b. 1809

Thursday
7

Alice James, b. 1848

Friday
8

Marjorie Kinnan Rawlings, b. 1896
Sara Teasdale, b. 1884

Saturday
9

July						
S	M	T	W	T	F	S
		1	2	3	4	5
6	7	8	9	10	11	12
13	14	15	16	17	18	19
20	21	22	23	24	25	26
27	28	29	30	31		

August
1997

September						
S	M	T	W	T	F	S
	1	2	3	4	5	6
7	8	9	10	11	12	13
14	15	16	17	18	19	20
21	22	23	24	25	26	27
28	29	30				

Sara Teasdale
(August 8, 1884 - January 29, 1933)

"You are a sharp arrow," wrote poet Vachel Lindsay.

Sara Teasdale's wealthy St. Louis family didn't think of her as an arrow—to them she was a frail flower, a delicate child whose first word was "pretty." Because of her fragile health, Sara was tutored at home until she was nine, freed from domestic chores, and allowed to spend a great deal of time reading and dreaming.

It was a beginning that produced one of America's finest lyric poets. It also produced a woman with a divided self—a Puritan and a Pagan, she called herself—a person who loved discipline and order and a passionate woman who erected a shrine to Aphrodite in her bedroom.

From the beginning of her career, Teasdale submitted her poetry to only the most prestigious magazines that published prominent male poets. She quickly won popular and critical acclaim. "Poetry has to have a certain smooth-flowing quality in order to be easily memorized," Teasdale felt, "and to be easily memorized is one of the reasons for poetry."

She also believed that a poem should spring "directly from the experience of the writer," like these lines from "Barter," her most famous poem:

> Spend all you have for loveliness,
> Buy it and never count the cost;
> For one white singing hour of peace
> Count many a year of strife well lost,
> And for a breath of ecstasy
> Give all you have been, or could be.

Courted by two men, the poet Vachel Lindsay and Ernest Filsinger, a businessman who knew most of her poems by heart, Teasdale married the businessman. "Be thankful two good men want you," her mother told her. "Remember some ain't got none." In 1929, Teasdale divorced her husband. "At last I am free!" she exclaimed. Her deepest and happiest relationships seem to have been with women. But she proclaimed in her poetry, "It was myself that sang in me."

On a trip to England, Teasdale became ill with bronchial pneumonia. When she returned to New York, she grew depressed and concerned that she might suffer a stroke. On the night before her death, she listened to Beethoven's Fifth Symphony with her companion Margaret Conklin. After she sent Conklin home, sometime during the night she filled the bathtub with water, swallowed a quantity of sleeping pills, and lay down in the tub.

Mary Roberts Rinehart
(August 12, 1876 - September 22, 1958)

In her first year as a professional writer, Mary Roberts Rinehart sold 45 stories and earned $1800.42. She worked quickly, grabbing "a few minutes here, a half hour there" from her duties as a mother and housewife. Lacking in craft, she resorted, she said, "to plot, that crutch of the beginner, that vice of the experienced writer."

She worked at a card table, writing in longhand and copying on a typewriter. She wore out a copy of Roget's *Thesaurus*. She never asked for or took an advance, preferring to sell only her completed work. Her first bestseller was *The Circular Staircase* (1908), followed the next year by *The Man in Lower Ten*. With Avery Hopwood she turned *The Circular Staircase* into *The Bat*, which had a long, lucrative run on Broadway.

Before her marriage to a physician, Rinehart worked as a nurse. In the hospital, she saw life at its "rawest and hardest." She wanted to write about the drama she saw all around her, to tell the truth about unfaithful husbands and ungrateful children, to record the "whirr of the bandage machine," and describe the intern who had rolled up his sleeve and sliced skin off his own arm for a burn victim. "But I could not write it," she said. "I have never written it."

As a child she had "no mad itch to express myself, but I liked words; I liked to sit down with a clean sheet of paper and put words on it." It took her many years, though, before she was able to tell the story of her childhood. In her autobiography she wrote of her inventor father, an unhappy dreamer who shot and killed himself while standing in front of his hotel room mirror just days before her wedding.

Looking back on her life, Rinehart found it curious that she had avoided realism in her stories and sought escape in tales of crime, adventure, and romance. In her own life and in her work as a nurse, she had seen "human relations at their most naked," but she would not disappoint her large and loyal audience by writing about a sordid, ugly reality. She would amuse and thrill her audience, she said, "but I would not pander to it."

In Rinehart's stories virtue triumphs and crime is punished. Just after one of her last books was published, her sons composed a jingle:

> And so your offspring, on this Mother's Day,
> Do homage to your homicidal knowledge.
> Who says that bloody murder does not pay?
> It helped to put the lot of us through college!

Sunday
10

 Monday
11

Louise Bogan, b. 1897

Tuesday
12

Edith Hamilton, b. 1867
Mary Roberts Rinehart, b. 1876

Wednesday
13

Thursday
14

Friday
15

Edna Ferber, b. 1855
Sir Walter Scott, b. 1771
Thomas De Quincey, b. 1785

Saturday
16

July						
S	M	T	W	T	F	S
		1	2	3	4	5
6	7	8	9	10	11	12
13	14	15	16	17	18	19
20	21	22	23	24	25	26
27	28	29	30	31		

August
1997

September						
S	M	T	W	T	F	S
	1	2	3	4	5	6
7	8	9	10	11	12	13
14	15	16	17	18	19	20
21	22	23	24	25	26	27
28	29	30				

Sunday
17

Monday
18

Elsa Morante, b. 1918

Tuesday
19

Ogden Nash, b. 1902

Wednesday
20

Thursday
21

Friday
22

Dorothy Parker, b. 1893

Saturday
23

Edgar Lee Masters, b. 1868

July						
S	M	T	W	T	F	S
		1	2	3	4	5
6	7	8	9	10	11	12
13	14	15	16	17	18	19
20	21	22	23	24	25	26
27	28	29	30	31		

August
1997

September						
S	M	T	W	T	F	S
	1	2	3	4	5	6
7	8	9	10	11	12	13
14	15	16	17	18	19	20
21	22	23	24	25	26	27
28	29	30				

Elsa Morante
(August 18, 1918 - November 25, 1985)

The year before her death, Elsa Morante confessed that only three things had ever mattered to her. "Love, children, and cats ... The people I have loved the most were children who had the eyes of a Siamese cat!"

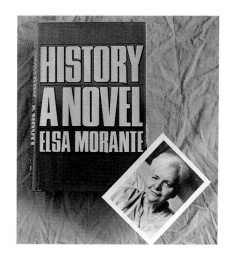

When her beloved cat Giuseppe died in 1952, Morante resolved never to be without a cat again. Giuseppe had been her best friend, she said. He was "half my soul." In a poem about another of her cats she wrote, "If I think of how many centuries and things separate us, I am frightened."

It was Morante's habit to turn the everyday facts of her life into the fantasy of fiction and poetry. "My desire to write was born with me," she declared. She began composing stories at the age of two-and-a-half; on the title page of one of her preschool notebooks she wrote: "Elsa Morante. My first book. It tells the story of a doll." By the time she was 13, Morante was publishing tales in children's magazines—and getting paid for it.

School bored her, as did the mundane conventions of everyday life. At meals she would sit down and announce, "I'm hungry. I'm going to eat. I'm not waiting for anyone." At the age of 18 she quit school, left her family, and began to earn a living by giving private Italian and Latin lessons in Rome and writing theses for university students. By 20 she was publishing her work in prominent Italian periodicals.

She married fellow novelist Alberto Moravia in 1941. (While kneeling at the altar during their wedding ceremony, Moravia heard the guests behind him discussing the siege of Stalingrad.) During the war Morante wrote her first major novel, *The House of Liars*, based on a tale she had heard about an old blind woman.

The book won Italy's prestigious Viareggio prize. Morante's fame grew. With the publication of her subsequent novels, *Arturo's Island* (1957) and *History: A Novel* (1974)—in which Morante painted a nightmare landscape of World War II Rome— she became a celebrity.

In her last novel, *Aracoeli*, Morante wrote of a character who suffered from hydrocephalus, an abnormal increase of fluid in the cranium. Two years after she finished the book, she was herself diagnosed with the disease. She spent the last years of her life in a hospital. Eight months before her death, Morante told a friend she wanted to write another novel. "The whole thing is in my head," she said. "Maybe that's why I'll never write it."

Bret Harte
(August 25, 1836 - May 5, 1902)

His name has a Western ring, evoking
a cardsharp in a crowded saloon or a
black-garbed gunslinger riding into
Dodge. Actually, Bret Harte was an
Eastern dandy from Albany, New York.
The son of a Greek scholar and a literary
critic, 12-year-old Bret wrote "Autumn
Musings" and never forgot the thrill of
seeing his poem published on the front
page of a New York journal.

Thinking of himself as a hero out of myth,
at 17 he left the East and traveled to the
gold fields of California by way of Panama.
"The setting was itself heroic," he wrote. "The great mountains of the Sierra Nevada
lifted majestic snow-capped peaks against a sky of purest blue." He married and
settled in San Francisco, where he supported himself working as private secretary to
the superintendent of the U.S. Mint. His real occupation was writing stories and
publishing and editing the *Overland Monthly*, which he turned into a west coast
Atlantic Monthly.

One day Samuel Clemens, who had been on a newspaper assignment in the mining
towns, dropped into his office and drawled out an irresistible story. Harte urged him
to write the tale down, offered critical advice, and the resoundingly successful *The
Notorious Jumping Frog of Calaveras County* was born. In his own stories and
sketches, like *The Luck of Roaring Camp*, *The Outcasts of Poker Flat*, and *The
Idyll of Red Gulch*, Harte transformed the wild, untamed west into a literary,
picturesque landscape.

In 1871, Harte became the most popular writer in America because of a 60-line dialect
poem about a "Heathen Chinee" who gets the best of two Westerners. Harte wrote the
poem quickly, threw it away, and then scavenged it out of the waste basket to use as
filler for the *Overland Monthly*. The poem created, said Mark Twain, "an explosion
of delight whose reverberations reached the last confines of Christendom."

Harte moved his family triumphantly east. The progress of their train was reported
hourly. People lined the streets, and celebrities competed to honor him. Later, Mark
Twain remarked that the train might as well have been Harte's funeral cortege since
"he had lived all his life that was worth living."

Harte never returned to California. Plagued by debts and unable to support himself
by writing, he took a position as U. S. Consul in Germany and later in Glasgow. He
spent his last years in London.

Wearing the costume of a British fop—monocle, cutaway coat, lavender spats, and
yellow gloves—Harte performed for London society. "I grind out the old tunes
and gather up the coppers," he said. He died of throat cancer.

Sunday
24

Monday
25

Tuesday
26

Wednesday
27

Thursday
28

Friday
29

Saturday
30

July						
S	M	T	W	T	F	S
		1	2	3	4	5
6	7	8	9	10	11	12
13	14	15	16	17	18	19
20	21	22	23	24	25	26
27	28	29	30	31		

August
1997

September						
S	M	T	W	T	F	S
	1	2	3	4	5	6
7	8	9	10	11	12	13
14	15	16	17	18	19	20
21	22	23	24	25	26	27
28	29	30				

Sunday

31

William Saroyan, b. 1908

Monday

1

Edgar Rice Burroughs, b. 1875
Labor Day

Tuesday

2

Wednesday

3

Sarah Orne Jewett, b. 1849

Thursday

4

Richard Wright, b. 1908
Antonin Artaud, b. 1896

Friday

5

Saturday

6

July						
S	M	T	W	T	F	S
		1	2	3	4	5
6	7	8	9	10	11	12
13	14	15	16	17	18	19
20	21	22	23	24	25	26
27	28	29	30	31		

August/September
1997

September						
S	M	T	W	T	F	S
	1	2	3	4	5	6
7	8	9	10	11	12	13
14	15	16	17	18	19	20
21	22	23	24	25	26	27
28	29	30				

On the Road

Henry Ford sold 10,067 cars the first year he put his mass-produced Model-T automobile on the market. Eight years later, annual sales of the Model-T exceeded 730,000. With a single stroke Ford had transformed the American landscape.

"The American really loves nothing but his automobile," said William Faulkner, who was one of many American writers to explore the car's omnipresent role in American life.

Even before Ford launched his first Model-T, Americans were fascinated by technology and its power to mold their lives. As an old man, Henry Adams stood before a display of electrical generators at the Great Exposition of 1900 and, in his words, "began to feel the forty-foot dynamos as a moral force, much as the early Christians felt the cross ... Before the end, one began to pray to it."

In the most famous of American automobile epics, Jack Kerouac's *On the Road*, the car inspires a similar kind of reverence. As Dean Moriarty and Sal Paradiso barrel down the highway in a "big, scarred, prophetic" Cadillac, Sal envisions the road beneath him, "unfurling and flying and hissing at incredible speeds across the groaning continent with that mad Ahab at the wheel."

To the young Californians in Tom Wolfe's *The Kandy* Kolored Tangerine* Flake Streamline Baby*, cars are objects of veneration signifying "freedom, style, sex, power, motion, color." To the Joad family in Steinbeck's *The Grapes of Wrath*, the ancient Hudson into which they sink their life earnings is both a monster and a messiah promising the dream of new life.

For Jay Gatsby the car is a death trap; for Hazel Motes, the hero of Flannery O'Connor's *Wise Blood*, it is a house. The sterile aristocrats in Eliot's *The Wasteland* arrive in "closed cars." Young Rufus Follet mourns the death of his father in a car accident in James Agee's *A Death in the Family*; Agee's book includes a page-and-a-half description of the car's doomed departure.

The list goes on. Thomas Pynchon, e. e. cummings, Norman Mailer, John Updike, Vladimir Nabokov, Booth Tarkington, Arthur Miller, Sinclair Lewis, Theodore Dreiser, John Dos Passos, and Edith Wharton have all written about cars and their enduring grip on the American imagination.

Two years after Ford sold his first Model-T, a man named Victor Appleton, Jr., published the first of his Tom Swift books—about an archetypal American tinkerer who wins fame and fortune by building cars. We have been dreaming about the automobile ever since.

Elinor Wylie
(September 7, 1885 - December 16, 1928)

She yearned to be as good a poet as Percy Bysshe Shelley. She was only seven when she first discovered him, and her obsession with Shelley and his work never faded. She used some of her first royalties to purchase a few of his letters. At dinner parties she argued his merits. She wrote two novels about him and dedicated her third volume of poetry to him, and in a sonnet sequence celebrating Shelley she confessed:

> If I possessed the pure and fiery pulse
> By true divinity informed and driven,
> I would unroll the rounded moon and sun
> And knit them up for you to walk upon.

But Elinor Wylie knew as well as anyone that she lacked her idol's prowess. She was, as she put it, a minor writer with a "small clean technique." She could create a "gilded bird" but not the living bird who sings in works of true genius.

Nonetheless, she wrote—poems, novels, essays, reviews. For long periods of time she composed a poem every morning. Her technical command was dazzling.

She had a perfectionist's drive for detail and a scholar's zeal for accuracy. When she worked on her novels—all of which were historical—she sat at a desk strewn with encyclopedias, reference books, and atlases.

Her poems and books earned Wylie modest acclaim, and in the 1920s she captivated the New York literary world with her sleek beauty and caustic wit. But beneath her elegant facade she was a mass of self-doubt and thwarted desire. Wylie married three times but failed to find happiness. She had several miscarriages, one stillbirth, and a premature child who died after a week. Her long and public affair with a married man scandalized much of the high society into which she was born.

Her redemption was writing. The older she became, the harder she worked. From 1921 to 1928 she turned out four volumes of poetry, four novels, and numerous essays and reviews. On the evening of December 16, 1928, in the midst of arranging poems for her newest collection, Wylie put down her typescript and asked her husband for a glass of water. As he brought it to her, she walked toward him and muttered, "Is that all it is?" An instant later she fell to the floor, dead from a stroke at the age of 43.

Sunday
7
Elinor Wylie, b. 1885

Monday
8

Fathers' Day (N.Z.)

 Tuesday
9

Leo Tolstoy, b. 1828
Wednesday
10

Hilda Doolittle, (H.D.), b. 1886
Thursday
11

D.H. Lawrence, b. 1885
O. Henry, b. 1862
Friday
12

Saturday
13
Roald Dahl, b. 1916

August						
S	M	T	W	T	F	S
					1	2
3	4	5	6	7	8	9
10	11	12	13	14	15	16
17	18	19	20	21	22	23
24	25	26	27	28	29	30
31						

September
1997

October						
S	M	T	W	T	F	S
			1	2	3	4
5	6	7	8	9	10	11
12	13	14	15	16	17	18
19	20	21	22	23	24	25
26	27	28	29	30	31	

Sunday
14

Monday
15

Agatha Christie, b. 1890
James Fenimore Cooper, b. 1789

Tuesday
16

Wednesday
17

William Carlos Williams, b. 1883

Thursday
18

Samuel Johnson, b. 1709

Friday
19

Saturday
20

Stevie Smith, b. 1902   Upton Sinclair, b. 1879

| August |
S M T W T F S
1 2
3 4 5 6 7 8 9
10 11 12 13 14 15 16
17 18 19 20 21 22 23
24 25 26 27 28 29 30
31

September
1997

| October |
S M T W T F S
1 2 3 4
5 6 7 8 9 10 11
12 13 14 15 16 17 18
19 20 21 22 23 24 25
26 27 28 29 30 31

James Fenimore Cooper
(September 15, 1789 - September 14, 1851)

One evening in the early 1800s, James Fenimore Cooper sat reading the latest English novel aloud to his wife. After just a few chapters, he flung it aside and announced, "I could write you a better book than that myself." Since his wife knew that he hated to write even a letter, she challenged him to prove it. After tearing up his first attempt, Cooper wrote *Precaution*, modeled after Jane Austen's *Persuasion*.

The novel was published anonymously, which was just as well since it was riddled with typesetting mistakes and populated with wooden characters. Despite these flaws, the book had a few good reviews in important British papers. Encouraged, Cooper quickly dashed off *The Spy*, writing as much as 30 pages a day. Published in December 1821 and widely translated, the book proved popular, especially with Europeans, who found that they liked reading about America.

Two years later when his third novel, *The Pioneers*, appeared in bookstores, 3,500 copies sold on the first day. It was the beginning of *The Leather-Stocking Tales*—a five-novel series about the pioneer scout Natty Bumppo that included *The Deerslayer*, *The Last of the Mohicans*, *The Pathfinder*, and *The Prairie*. Later Philip Rahv pointed out "one suspects that Hemingway, that perennial boy-man, is more accurately understood as a descendant of Natty Bumppo."

Cooper composed in his head as he walked or lay in bed. He wrote at set hours every day, and what actually got on paper, he said, was largely a matter of chance. While some felt that Cooper was at his best describing "the delicate art of the forest," Mark Twain complained that "every time a Cooper person is in peril, and absolute silence is worth four dollars a minute, he is sure to step on a dry twig ... the Leatherstocking Series ought to have been called the Broken Twig Series." In *The Deerslayer*, said Twain, in just two thirds of a page, Cooper "scored 114 offenses against literary art out of a possible 115."

Cooper knew little about art. He had entered Yale at 13, "a fine sparkling beautiful boy," said one of his teachers, but was expelled for exploding gunpowder and placing a donkey in a professor's chair. He hacked his way through the literary thickets alone, the first American writer to achieve worldwide readership. Like Natty Bumppo, he blazed the trail for those who would follow.

H. G. Wells
(September 21, 1866 - August 13, 1946)

He was a pale, undernourished boy with bright blue eyes, trapped in a murky world. He drudged along with his mother in their basement kitchen beneath his father's glass and china shop. "Woman is destined for man's slave," Sarah Wells wrote in her diary. Her youngest son, Herbert George Wells, longed to change the world that enslaved women and enforced a rigid social order.

When he was 14, Wells worked 70 hours a week as an apprentice in a drapery shop. "Time here is wasted," he wrote Sarah Wells. "It would be the kindest and wisest thing you could do now to let me leave here very soon." For a time, he lived with his mother at a large house in Sussex, called Up Park, where she toiled as a chambermaid and lived mostly underground in the estate's dank tunnels and dingy cellars.

Education was his salvation. He earned a scholarship to London University, where he studied with scientist Thomas Huxley. "The years of intellectual starvation," wrote Wells's biographer Lovatt Dickson, "had left him with such an appetite for learning that he felt he could never read enough."

For several years, Wells taught school, but his real passion was writing. His first book, *The Time Machine* (1895), which told the story of the Morlocks—half-human creatures who toiled in underground caverns, and the childlike Eloi who lived carelessly in the sun—drew on his childhood memories of British class divisions. The book was an overwhelming success, quickly followed by *The War of the Worlds*, *The Invisible Man*, *The Island of Dr. Moreau*, and *The First Men in the Moon*. "Literature is illumination, the salvation of ourselves, and everyone," he believed.

His literary output was astonishing. He invented the genre of science fiction, wrote realistic novels and utopian tracts, using literature not as an artistic end, but as a means to save society. "My Drive goes on when I am worked out," he wrote, "It is a race against death." Not everyone welcomed his efforts. "I stopped thinking about him," said Lytton Strachey, "when he became a thinker."

Disillusioned by World War I, Wells decided to write a book "that will twist the minds of its readers round towards a new set of values." Titled *The Outline of History*, the work sold millions of copies, but Wells saw no sign that society had been changed.

Still, he remained optimistic. "Worlds may freeze and suns may perish," he said, "but I believe there stirs something within us now that can never die again."

Sunday
21
H.G.Wells, b. 1866

Monday
22

Fall Equinox, 7:57 pm EDT

 Tuesday
23

Wednesday
24

Frances Ellen Watkins Harper, b. 1825 [?]

Thursday
25

Red Smith, b.1905
William Faulkner, b. 1897

Friday
26

Saturday
27
Grazia Deledda, b. 1871

August						
S	M	T	W	T	F	S
					1	2
3	4	5	6	7	8	9
10	11	12	13	14	15	16
17	18	19	20	21	22	23
24	25	26	27	28	29	30
31						

September
1997

October						
S	M	T	W	T	F	S
			1	2	3	4
5	6	7	8	9	10	11
12	13	14	15	16	17	18
19	20	21	22	23	24	25
26	27	28	29	30	31	

Sunday
28

Monday
29

Miguel de Unamuno, b. 1864
Miguel De Cervantes Saavedra, b. 1547
Elizabeth Gaskell, b. 1810

Tuesday
30

Truman Capote, b. 1924

Wednesday
1

Rosh Hashanah begins at sunset, Hebrew Year 5758

Thursday
2

Wallace Stevens, b. 1879

Friday
3

Thomas Wolfe, b. 1900

Saturday
4

Edward Stratemeyer, b. 1862   Damon Runyon, b. 1884

August						
S	M	T	W	T	F	S
					1	2
3	4	5	6	7	8	9
10	11	12	13	14	15	16
17	18	19	20	21	22	23
24	25	26	27	28	29	30
31						

September/October
1997

October						
S	M	T	W	T	F	S
			1	2	3	4
5	6	7	8	9	10	11
12	13	14	15	16	17	18
19	20	21	22	23	24	25
26	27	28	29	30	31	

Miguel de Unamuno
(September 29, 1864 - December 31, 1936)

Every day after teaching, Miguel de
Unamuno, professor of Greek language
and literature at the University of Salamanca
as well as rector of the institution, spent two
hours doing administrative work before
eating his lunch. After lunch he took a siesta,
wrote articles or essays, and then went for
a long walk through the old Spanish city
whose sights and sounds he revered.

He was disciplined to a fault, and the results
were astounding. He once completed a
sonnet cycle of 128 poems in four months'
time. Besides poetry, Unamuno wrote
essays, novels, articles, travel sketches,
plays, and books of philosophy. He loomed
so large in the world of turn-of-the-century
Spanish letters that one of his contemporaries called him the rector "not only
of Salamanca" but of Spain itself.

He dressed like a Protestant minister, in a dark, high-buttoned suit and vest, white
shirt, and small round hat. He had an aquiline nose, a barbed goatee, and round,
wire-rimmed spectacles that gave him the appearance of an owl.

But though he looked like a minister, Unamuno lacked a minister's conviction. At
14 he underwent a profound spiritual crisis and subsequently lost what he called the
"serene intuition" of his childhood faith. Throughout his life Unamuno kept track of
his spiritual evolution, often by writing poems.

In his controversial 1913 masterpiece, *The Tragic Sense of Life*, Unamuno explored
the universal human fixation on death and questioned the existence of God. Suffering,
he suggested, is the essence of life.

In his own life he knew tremendous suffering. Because of his outspoken liberal
politics he was banished from Spain in 1923 and spent the next seven years in exile
in France, where he was convinced he would die. With the onset of the Spanish
Republic in 1930, Unamuno returned to Spain in triumph. But his jubilation was
short-lived. Within three years his country was in a state of political chaos. In
1936, civil war broke out.

Unamuno denounced the Spanish Civil War and decried the politics of General
Francisco Franco. Franco ordered him shot. But, fearing a public relations debacle,
the General's troops instead placed Unamuno under strict house arrest. In the confines
of his home in Salamanca, his heart shattered by the events that had befallen his
country, Unamuno quietly withered. On New Year's Eve, 1936, six months after
the start of the Civil War, he died.

Eleanor Roosevelt
(October 11, 1884 - November 7, 1962)

She was a Roosevelt—daughter of Elliott,
niece of Theodore, wife of Franklin, mother
of five Roosevelt children. Yet, writes Blanche
Wiesen Cook in her ground-breaking biography, Eleanor Roosevelt was her own woman—
"a woman who insists on her right to self-
identity, a woman who creates herself over
and over again, a woman of consummate
power and courageous vision ..."

Tall and long-legged, with luxuriant golden
hair, blue eyes, and a dazzling smile that
revealed protruding teeth, Eleanor Roosevelt
confused observers. Some thought her ugly;
some declared that she was beautiful and
"her very presence lit up the room." On her
honeymoon with FDR, when they went to the
beach, she wore a skirt, a long-sleeved, high-
necked blouse, stockings, and gloves, a carry-
over from the Victorian Age. But Eleanor
Roosevelt was not a Victorian lady.

She was a humanist. Before her marriage to FDR, she was already active in various
social causes. After he was stricken with polio, she involved herself in politics, civil
rights, and women's groups. Encouraged by her close friend Lorena Hickok, a top
reporter for the Associated Press, in 1935 Eleanor began writing a daily newspaper
column that was syndicated nationwide. She could be scathing in her criticism. "A
trait no other nation seems to possess in quite the same degree that we do," she wrote,
"namely, a feeling of almost childish injury and resentment unless the world as a
whole recognizes how innocent we are of anything but the most generous and
harmless intentions."

Her outspokenness earned her the enmity of J. Edgar Hoover, who kept a file of her
"every word and activity" from 1924 until her death. Her ambitions were attacked, and
she was condemned for wearing plain hats and "ten dollar dresses," for her custom of
traveling alone on public transportation, and even for buying apples
from street stands.

Secure in her beliefs, she laughed at the ridiculous charges. As a schoolgirl, Eleanor
had defended ambition because "it seems to be a great good for it leads one to do, and
to be things which without it one could never have been." After FDR's death, she
devoted herself to human rights around the world. She published a number of books,
including *It's Up to the Women*, *This Troubled World*, *The Moral Basis of Democracy*,
This Is My Story, and her 1961 autobiography.

In her last book, she wrote, "There is no more liberating, no more exhilarating
experience than to determine one's position, state it bravely and then act boldly."

Sunday
5

Monday
6

Tuesday
7

Wednesday
8

 Thursday
9

Friday
10

Yom Kippur begins at sunset

Saturday
11

September						
S	M	T	W	T	F	S
	1	2	3	4	5	6
7	8	9	10	11	12	13
14	15	16	17	18	19	20
21	22	23	24	25	26	27
28	29	30				

October
1997

November						
S	M	T	W	T	F	S
						1
2	3	4	5	6	7	8
9	10	11	12	13	14	15
16	17	18	19	20	21	22
23	24	25	26	27	28	29
30						

Sunday

12

Monday

13

Columbus Day
Thanksgiving Day (Canada)

Tuesday

14

Hannah Arendt, b. 1906
Katherine Mansfield, b. 1888
e. e. cummings, b. 1894

Wednesday

15

Virgil, b. 70 B.C.

Thursday

16

Oscar Wilde, b. 1854
Eugene O'Neill, b. 1888
Noah Webster, b. 1758

Friday

17

Saturday

18

September						
S	M	T	W	T	F	S
	1	2	3	4	5	6
7	8	9	10	11	12	13
14	15	16	17	18	19	20
21	22	23	24	25	26	27
28	29	30				

October
1997

November						
S	M	T	W	T	F	S
						1
2	3	4	5	6	7	8
9	10	11	12	13	14	15
16	17	18	19	20	21	22
23	24	25	26	27	28	29
30						

Hannah Arendt
(October 14, 1906 - December 4, 1975)

Shortly after the burning of the Reichstag in 1933, Hannah Arendt, a 26-year-old German Jew, was arrested by Hitler's police and held for questioning at police headquarters in Berlin for eight days. Throughout the ordeal, Arendt said nothing to incriminate herself or the German Zionist Organization for whom she had recently begun to work. She even persuaded a policeman to get her cigarettes and to improve the quality of the coffee. Released unharmed, Arendt promptly fled Germany with her mother.

"I wanted to do practical work," she said later of her life during the war years. "Exclusively and only Jewish work."

In Paris, where she first sought refuge, Arendt served for a time as general secretary to a Jewish refugee organization. Following the Nazi invasion of France, she and her second husband, Heinrich Blücher, whom she had met in Paris, escaped to New York, where they were to remain for the rest of their lives. Arendt arrived in the United States knowing no English except for two Shakespeare sonnets. By 1944 she was writing articles in English for the *Partisan Review*.

Although her training was in philosophy (in Germany she had been both the student and the lover of Martin Heidegger), Arendt renounced any claim to being a philosopher. She was a profound and original thinker nonetheless, whose books and articles run the gamut from philosophy to biography to political theory. Each of her books builds on ideas introduced in its predecessor.

Two issues dominate Arendt's writing: the problem of political evil in the 20th century and the dilemma of the Jew in the contemporary world. In one of her best known and most controversial works, *Eichmann in Jerusalem*, Arendt coined the unforgettable phrase "the banality of evil" to describe Adolf Eichmann and his ilk. She wrote the book, she later said, "in a curious state of euphoria."

An inveterate smoker with a fondness for pipes and cigars as well as cigarettes, Arendt was possessed of a restless, decisive spirit. Even while giving a lecture, remembered her close friend Mary McCarthy, Arendt's feet "seemed to keep pace with her thought."

On December 4, 1975, while serving dinner to two guests in her Manhattan apartment, Arendt suffered a heart attack. She died that evening without regaining consciousness. In her typewriter sat the first page of the final section of her latest book, *The Life of the Mind*. Arendt had typed a title—"Judging"—and was waiting to begin the rest.

Found in Translation

If you think of languages as rivers flowing parallel to one another, says poet and translator Richard Howard, then translations are the bridges that "help us to get from one river to the other." But the bridge, Howard reminds, "is not the same thing as the river."

Inevitably things get lost in translation—words, idioms, puns, rhymes, cultural and literary allusions. A work's "interior" can disappear, says poet Robert Bly. "Poetry," said Robert Frost, "is what gets lost in translation."

At its worst, translation can mar one's appreciation of an original work. Of Gilbert Murray's grandiloquent attempt at rendering *Medea* in English, T. S. Eliot complained that it "raised between Euripides and ourselves a barrier more impenetrable than the Greek language."

But while literary purists may insist that no work can effectively be translated, Edith Hamilton argues in the introduction to her translation of three Greek plays that "unless we do try, something unique and never surpassed will cease to exist except in the libraries of a few inquisitive book lovers."

The challenges of translation have tantalized many authors. Coleridge labored over the dense German of Schiller's dramas. Ezra Pound translated Chinese, Anglo-Saxon, Provençal, Greek, and Italian poetry into English and in the process discovered new directions for his own work.

For Louise Bogan, the act of translating poems by Rilke and Heine was a "means of remaining open to creative impulses when they otherwise chose to retreat or even disappear," writes her biographer Elizabeth Frank. During the 1960s the Iowa Poetry Workshop placed great emphasis on translation. Workshop directors Paul Engle and Donald Justice urged students with foreign language backgrounds to undertake translation work during bouts of writer's block.

At its best, translation revolutionizes our understanding of the world. Rolf Fjelde, acclaimed for his translations of Ibsen, remembers sitting in the audience in 1955 during the first New York production of Richard Wilbur's brilliant new translation of Molière. "It was as if a bright, clarifying light had been switched on in a dark and musty warehouse filled with old cultural baggage."

To Fjelde, translation is "a unicorn in the menagerie of the arts." More so perhaps than any other art, translation reminds us that we speak a common language. As Aristotle observed, "Though writing and the spoken word are not the same for all men, the states of soul and the things that these signs designate are the same."

Sunday
19

Monday
20

Tuesday
21

Wednesday
22

 Thursday
23

Friday
24

Saturday
25

September						
S	M	T	W	T	F	S
	1	2	3	4	5	6
7	8	9	10	11	12	13
14	15	16	17	18	19	20
21	22	23	24	25	26	27
28	29	30				

October
1997

November						
S	M	T	W	T	F	S
						1
2	3	4	5	6	7	8
9	10	11	12	13	14	15
16	17	18	19	20	21	22
23	24	25	26	27	28	29
30						

Sunday
26
Daylight Saving Time ends

Monday
27

Sylvia Plath, b. 1932
Dylan Thomas, b. 1914
Labour Day (N.Z.)

Tuesday
28

Evelyn Waugh, b. 1903

Wednesday
29

James Boswell, b. 1740
Jean Giraudoux, b. 1882

Thursday
30

Ezra Pound, b. 1885

Friday
31

John Keats, b. 1795
Halloween

Saturday
1
Stephen Crane, b. 1871

September						
S	M	T	W	T	F	S
	1	2	3	4	5	6
7	8	9	10	11	12	13
14	15	16	17	18	19	20
21	22	23	24	25	26	27
28	29	30				

October/November
1997

November						
S	M	T	W	T	F	S
						1
2	3	4	5	6	7	8
9	10	11	12	13	14	15
16	17	18	19	20	21	22
23	24	25	26	27	28	29
30						

James Boswell
(October 29, 1740 - May 19, 1795)

"If you have a mean, pedantic spirit," observed Frank Brady, James Boswell's biographer, "you will write a mean, pedantic biography." Only Boswell, Brady argues, "with his acute intelligence, his brilliant technique, and his open loving heart," could fully realize Samuel Johnson's greatness.

James Boswell shared his biographer's opinion of his worth. About his *Life of Johnson*, Boswell told Fanny Burney, "There's nothing like it; there never was; and there never will be!" But Boswell also could laugh at himself. "There have been many people who built castles in the air," he wrote, "but I believe I am the first that ever attempted to live in them."

Urged to study law by Lord Auchinleck, his domineering father, Boswell did become a lawyer, but his real genius lay in writing. "Words cannot describe our feelings," he said. "The finer parts are lost, as the down upon a plum." Yet he was adept at articulating emotion. "I just sat and hugged myself in my own mind," he wrote.

On May 16, 1763, Boswell met Samuel Johnson, and became part of a circle that included the greatest male minds of the 18th century—including Edmund Burke, David Garrick, and Joshua Reynolds. In preparing his biography of Johnson, Boswell felt that he had to be "exact as to every line in his countenance, every hair, every mole." He recorded Johnson's conversations, traveled with him, and checked and rechecked his facts. When asked by Mrs. Thrale to suppress Johnson's flaws, Boswell replied that he would "not make a tiger a cat to please anybody."

In his own time, some derided Boswell as a fool and a gossip, a drunk and a whore-monger, a sort of 18th-century celebrity journalist who told the truth about the famous. "Curiosity carried Boswell farther than it ever carried any mortal breathing," said Mrs. Thrale. He was the first modern literary biographer, and his genius at recreating a life has yet to be equaled.

"I surely have the art of writing agreeably," said an uncharacteristically modest Boswell.

Albert Camus
(November 7, 1913 - January 4, 1960)

That one of the greatest writers and
thinkers of the 20th century grew up
fatherless and poor in a silent home in
Algiers, without books, magazines, or
newspapers, seems the stuff of fiction.

His mother rarely spoke and his
stern grandmother beat him with a
dried ligament from a bull's neck.
Still, Albert Camus remembered
his childhood as filled with joy.
The blazing North African sun, the pounding surf of the Mediterranean, his love
for his mother, and the encouragement of a gifted teacher all combined to create
a humanist possessed by the beauty as well as the absurdity of the world.

In 1942, Camus, not yet 30, worked on three projects simultaneously—a novel,
The Stranger; a play, *Caligula*; and an essay, *The Myth of Sisyphus*. In his writing,
he articulated and defined the feelings of an age gripped by world war and mass
murder. Without illusions and without light, "man feels a stranger," Camus wrote.
"This divorce between man and his life ... truly constitutes the feeling of Absurdity."

A tall, elegant man, Camus gave few interviews and rarely discussed his writing
habits. He jotted down thoughts, quotations, and ideas for future work in a small
student notebook. About an adverse review, he said, "Three years to write a book,
five lines to ridicule it." He urged himself to "write everything—just as it comes."

In 1957, he received the Nobel Prize. The timing was ironic. He could not write,
and he questioned his future as a writer. "I'm castrated," he said. "Serves him
right," sniped his enemies.

With the $42,000 prize money, he bought a house in southern France and was able
to overcome his writer's block. He wrote 145 pages of an autobiographical novel
about a poor boy in Algiers who had "to learn by himself, to grow alone, in fortitude,
in strength, find his own morality and truth, at last to be born as a man."

While he was driving to Paris one drizzly January day, Camus was killed instantly
when the Facel Vega sports car he was riding in veered off the road and crashed into
a tree. His black leather briefcase containing his unfinished novel was found in the
road. Titled *The First Man*, it was finally published in France in 1994 and in the
United States in 1995 to critical acclaim.

Sunday
2

Monday
3

Tuesday
4

Ivan Sergeyevich Turgenev, b. 1816
Will Rogers, b. 1879
Election Day

Wednesday
5

Thursday
6

 Friday
7

Albert Camus, b. 1913

Saturday
8

Margaret Mitchell, b. 1900

October						
S	M	T	W	T	F	S
			1	2	3	4
5	6	7	8	9	10	11
12	13	14	15	16	17	18
19	20	21	22	23	24	25
26	27	28	29	30	31	

November
1997

December						
S	M	T	W	T	F	S
	1	2	3	4	5	6
7	8	9	10	11	12	13
14	15	16	17	18	19	20
21	22	23	24	25	26	27
28	29	30	31			

Sunday
9
Anne Sexton, b. 1928

Monday
10

Tuesday
11

Feodor Dostoevsky, b. 1821
Veterans' Day
Remembrance Day (Canada)

Wednesday
12

Sor Juana Inés de la Cruz, b. 1651
Elizabeth Cady Stanton, b. 1815

Thursday
13

Saint Augustine, b. 354

Friday
14

Canterbury Anniversary (N.Z.)

Saturday
15
Marianne Moore, b. 1887

October						
S	M	T	W	T	F	S
				1	2	3	4
5	6	7	8	9	10	11
12	13	14	15	16	17	18
19	20	21	22	23	24	25
26	27	28	29	30	31	

November
1997

December						
S	M	T	W	T	F	S
	1	2	3	4	5	6
7	8	9	10	11	12	13
14	15	16	17	18	19	20
21	22	23	24	25	26	27
28	29	30	31			

Elizabeth Cady Stanton
(November 12, 1815 - October 26, 1902)

Round and jolly in rustling black silk, with white lace covering her silver curls, and bright blue eyes in a sweet, round face, she was the picture of a Victorian lady. She was not. She was a modern revolutionary. For almost 50 years, Elizabeth Cady Stanton worked for the right of women to vote, to attend college, to enter professions, even to ride a bicycle.

Born into wealth in Jonestown, New York, Stanton was the seventh child in a family of girls. Her father wished for a son. She was a gifted scholar and excellent athlete—"of which my father would have felt a proper pride had I been a man," Stanton said.

Throughout her life, she used her full name. "The custom of calling women Mrs. John This and Mrs. Tom That and colored men Sambo and Zip Coon is founded on the principle that white men are the lords of all. I cannot acknowledge this principle as just; therefore I cannot bear the name of another."

When Stanton married abolitionist Henry Stanton, she cut the word "obey" from the ceremony. She gave birth to seven children, but she believed that those who created art or philosophy lived to a higher purpose than those "whose children are of the flesh alone." After attending the Seneca Falls convention for women's rights in 1848, Stanton began to promote her philosophy. With Susan B. Anthony, she wrote the three-volume *History of Woman Suffrage*, published numerous articles, and gave countless speeches.

When she thought "of all the wrongs that have been heaped upon womankind, I am ashamed that I am not forever in a condition of chronic wrath, stark mad, skin and bone, my eyes a fountain of tears, my lips overflowing with curses, and my hand against every man and his brother."

She poured her wrath into *The Woman's Bible*, which was published in two volumes in 1895 and 1898. With scholarship and sarcasm, she proclaimed a God who was both Mother and Father, and she charged the male clergy with using the Bible to degrade and repress women. A best seller, the book went through seven printings in six months. Stanton's attack on religion was denounced. Young feminists feared that she had hurt the cause.

In her comprehensive biography, Elisabeth Griffith observes that "Stanton was the first person to enumerate every major advance achieved for women in the last century and many of the reforms still on the agenda in this century." At times Stanton wondered, though, if it would ever be possible for one class of people to appreciate the wrongs of another.

Selma Lagerlöf
(November 20, 1858 - March 16, 1940)

All day long her grandmother would sit on
the corner sofa and tell stories, and Selma
Lagerlöf would listen. "It was a glorious
life," she remembered. Few children were
so blessed. And then, when Selma turned
five, her grandmother died. "It was as if the
door to a wonderful magic world, in and out
of which we had come and gone freely, had
been locked, and there was no one now
who knew how to open it."

But her grandmother's legacy endured. At
the age of seven Selma read her first novel—
Mayne Reid's *Oceola*—and resolved one day
"to produce something as fine." She became
a voracious reader and a passionate versifier.
At nine she saw her first theater and began
writing plays.

Unlike her brothers and sisters, who revelled in outdoor games on the family's
wooded estate in central Sweden, Selma played in a world of her own invention.
She had little choice. Paralyzed by a childhood illness, she did not walk alone until
she was five years old, and afterward she continued to suffer from a lame hip. Stories
became her life.

It was while studying to be a teacher in Stockholm that Selma Lagerlöf first saw the
direction her own writing must take. After hearing a lecture on Sweden's ancient epic
poems, she realized that the stories and folk tales she had heard in childhood contained
material every bit as rich as that of the old epics. Shortly afterward she began her first
novel, *Gosta Berling*, the saga of a charismatic former priest in 19th-century Sweden.
The book launched Lagerlöf's career.

She went on to write many more stories and books, including the children's classic,
The Wonderful Adventures of Nils. In 1909 she won the Nobel Prize—the first woman
and the first Swedish writer to do so. In her acceptance speech, Lagerlöf imagined
herself travelling to heaven in order to tell her father the extraordinary news of
her award.

As a child, Selma had adored her father. Every August she wrote poems and plays
for his birthday celebration. She was 26 when he died, and not yet known as a writer.
Shortly after his death, her mother was forced to sell the family estate. Nearly 30 years
later, with the money she had earned from her novels and from the Nobel Prize, Selma
Lagerlöf was able to buy back her childhood home. She lived out her years there,
surrounded by the woods and lakes and imaginary beings that had sparked
her imagination as a child and subsequently filled her books.

Sunday
16
George S. Kaufman, b. 1889

Monday
17

Tuesday
18

W. S. Gilbert, b. 1836
Wednesday
19

Thursday
20

Selma Lagerlöf, b. 1858
 ## Friday
21

Voltaire, b. 1694
Saturday
22
George Eliot, b. 1819

October						
S	M	T	W	T	F	S
				1	2	3	4
5	6	7	8	9	10	11
12	13	14	15	16	17	18
19	20	21	22	23	24	25
26	27	28	29	30	31	

November
1997

December						
S	M	T	W	T	F	S
	1	2	3	4	5	6
7	8	9	10	11	12	13
14	15	16	17	18	19	20
21	22	23	24	25	26	27
28	29	30	31			

Sunday
23

Monday
24

Tuesday
25

Lope de Vega, b. 1562

Wednesday
26

Eugene Ionesco, b. 1912

Thursday
27

Fanny Kemble, b. 1809
Thanksgiving Day

Friday
28

Saturday
29

C. S. Lewis, b. 1898   Louisa May Alcott, b. 1832

October						
S	M	T	W	T	F	S
				1	2	3	4
5	6	7	8	9	10	11
12	13	14	15	16	17	18
19	20	21	22	23	24	25
26	27	28	29	30	31	

November
1997

December						
S	M	T	W	T	F	S
	1	2	3	4	5	6
7	8	9	10	11	12	13
14	15	16	17	18	19	20
21	22	23	24	25	26	27
28	29	30	31			

Fanny Kemble
(November 27, 1809 - January 15, 1893)

A "disgusting travesty"—such was Frances
Anne Kemble's view of the theater. Acting,
she believed, eroded the personality. Still,
it earned her a living, and she devoted
much of her life to it.

Her real love was writing. She composed
plays and a travel diary in her youth, and
later wrote seven additional books. At 80
she published her first novel.

Her close friend Henry James noted that
Fanny Kemble wrote "exactly as she talked,
observing, asserting, complaining, confid-
ing, contradicting," and always "effectively
communicating." She never revised what
she wrote, and she harbored no delusions
about her stature as a writer. She wrote,
simply, because writing satisfied a deep need.

It was as an actress, however, that Kemble "literally coined money," as she phrased
it. Born into a distinguished British theater family (her aunt was Sarah Siddons),
Fanny Kemble was put onstage in London at the age of 20 in order to save her
father's waning fortunes, and she became an instant stage sensation.

Three years later, in 1832, she toured America. Her fame grew. Harvard students
lionized her; girls began wearing Fanny Kemble ringlets. In Philadelphia, Kemble
met Pierce Butler, heir to a Georgia rice plantation. The couple fell in love, married,
had two daughters in quick succession, and Kemble quit the stage, intent on
enjoying a quiet family life where she could write.

But her husband opposed her new vocation and sought to suppress the publication
of her first book, a journal of Kemble's reflections on America. The marriage deterio-
rated. When Kemble travelled to Georgia and saw the conditions in which her
husband's 700 plantation slaves lived, she was sickened. The record of her months
as a slaveowner's wife, *Journal of a Residence on a Georgian Plantation in 1838-39*,
was published during the American Civil War and helped bolster the abolitionist
cause. Henry James considered the work "easily the best" of Kemble's prose.

Kemble divorced her husband in 1849. In later years she made her name giving
readings of Shakespeare. A handsome, high-spirited woman with a boisterous laugh,
she received special praise for her interpretation of Falstaff. Henry James called her
"my sublime Fanny." In letters to James, Kemble referred to herself as "Your old
Gossip." When Kemble died in 1893, James confessed to Fanny's daughter, "I am
conscious of a strange bareness and a kind of evening chill, as it were, in the air, as
of some great object that had filled it for long and left an emptiness."

Jonathan Swift
(November 30, 1667 - October 19, 1745)

Torn between Ireland, "a land of slaves," and England, where he would have preferred to live, Jonathan Swift vented his rage at the world in sermons, pamphlets, and books. Devoted to reason and simple common sense, he loathed the stupidity and grossness of his fellow human beings who hid their diseases and corruptions under fashionable layers of lace and velvet, rouged their cheeks, and disguised their stinking body odors with perfume.

Born in Dublin, Swift was the son of an Englishman who died before he was born. The "younger son of younger sons," he depended on the charity of his uncles, who sent him to Trinity College when he was 14. He was a surly, somewhat indifferent scholar who longed to be famous.

With the publication of *A Tale of a Tub*, a scathing satire about religious excess, Swift achieved his ambition. "Good God! what a genius I had when I wrote that book," he exclaimed.

An Anglican priest, Swift spent most of his life as Dean of St. Patrick's Cathedral in Dublin. He ruled the Deanery with an iron hand. No matter was too small to escape his attention. "If one cannot mend the public, one had better mend old shoes," he said.

Although he disliked the Irish, Swift hated English oppression even more. He became an Irish national hero with the publication of *A Modest Proposal,* which advocated solving the problem of poverty in Ireland by selling the babies of the poor as food to feed the rich. "A young healthy child well nursed is at a year old a most delicious, nourishing, and wholesome food," he wrote.

His masterpiece was *Gulliver's Travels*. Ironically, this savage satire was sanitized into a popular children's book. Gulliver's journey, written in vivid, concrete language, has an irresistible appeal to readers of any age. A giant baby's wail sounds like "a squall that you might have heard from London Bridge to Chelsea," and wasps as large as partridges buzz like bagpipes.

After *Gulliver's Travels* was published in 1726, Swift restricted his writing to "bagatelles." In an age given to frippery in clothes and speech, Swift was a master of plain talk. "We have just enough religion to make us hate," he said, "but not enough to make us love one another." When true genius appeared, he wrote, "you may know him by this sign, that the dunces are all in confederacy against him."

He passed his last years in madness. "Where fierce indignation can no longer tear his heart," reads his epitaph.

Sunday
30

Jonathan Swift, b. 1667   Mark Twain, b. 1835   Lucy Maud Montgomery, b. 1874

Monday
1

Tuesday
2

Wednesday
3

Thursday
4

Rainer Maria Rilke, b. 1875

Friday
5

Saturday
6

Susannah Moodie, b. 1803

October						
S	M	T	W	T	F	S
			1	2	3	4
5	6	7	8	9	10	11
12	13	14	15	16	17	18
19	20	21	22	23	24	25
26	27	28	29	30	31	

November/December
1997

December						
S	M	T	W	T	F	S
	1	2	3	4	5	6
7	8	9	10	11	12	13
14	15	16	17	18	19	20
21	22	23	24	25	26	27
28	29	30	31			

Sunday
7

Pearl Harbor Day   *Willa Cather, b. 1873*

Monday
8

James Thurber, b. 1894

Tuesday
9

Wednesday
10

Emily Dickinson, b. 1830

Thursday
11

Friday
12

Gustave Flaubert, b. 1821

Saturday
13

November						
S	M	T	W	T	F	S
						1
2	3	4	5	6	7	8
9	10	11	12	13	14	15
16	17	18	19	20	21	22
23	24	25	26	27	28	29
30						

December
1997

January 1998						
S	M	T	W	T	F	S
				1	2	3
4	5	6	7	8	9	10
11	12	13	14	15	16	17
18	19	20	21	22	23	24
25	26	27	28	29	30	31

James Thurber
(December 8, 1894 - November 2, 1961)

During a game of William Tell with his
brothers, six-year-old Jamie Thurber took
his turn to be the target and stood against the
house. Just as his brother drew back the bow,
Jamie turned his head. The arrow struck his
left eye, damaging it irreversibly. The blind
eye was not removed for weeks, and by that
time the other eye had become inflamed.
With a glass left eye and deteriorating sight
in his right eye, James Thurber envisioned a
world and created a body of literature and
drawings that are immediately recognizable
as Thurber art.

Thurber's cartoons of aggressive women,
meek men, compliant dogs, and talking
seals have become classics. According to
his biographer Burton Bernstein, "Thurber not only pencilled odd pictures and
ominous phrases on office walls, he doodled on tablecloths, envelopes, and on reams
of copy paper, as a kind of tic or nervous habit, like biting one's fingernails." He gave
away his drawings "like smiles," Bernstein reports.

E. B. White, who shared a tiny office with Thurber at the *New Yorker*, plucked
Thurber's drawings and captions out of the wastebasket and submitted them to the
magazine. Hired first as an editor, Thurber missed deadlines on purpose, rolled water
bottles around the office, and made prank phone calls. An exasperated Harold Ross
told him, "I thought you were an editor, goddam it, but I guess you're a writer, so
write. Maybe you have something to say."

He did. *Is Sex Necessary?* he and E. B White asked in their spoof of sex manuals.
In *My Life and Hard Times*, Thurber drew on memories of growing up in Columbus,
Ohio, and transformed family calamities into outrageous comedies. Other books
followed, including *My World—and Welcome to It, The Thurber Carnival, Many
Moons*, and *The Last Flower*, which he composed at the beginning of World War II.
The Last Flower, a fable of a world destroyed by war except for one man, one
woman, and one flower, is deeply moving.

As he aged and his world turned dark, Thurber flew into rages, which his wife called
"Thurbs." He continued to work, though, dictating his words to a secretary and
drawing with the aid of a Zeiss loop which made him look, he said, "like a welder
from Mars."

Thurber once told E. B. White that he wrote humor "the way a surgeon operates."
White disagreed. "Thurber did not write the way a surgeon operates," said White,
"he wrote the way a child skips rope, the way a mouse waltzes."

Ford Madox Ford
(December 17, 1873 - June 26, 1939)

"Ford was a character," remembered fellow author Malcolm Cowley. "He was a liar, not for his own profit, but just because he had a very faint hold on actuality. He told beautiful stories of English literary life, in which he knew everybody, had a hand in everything, and his hand grew larger as he told the story."

Others who knew Ford Madox Ford—and his penchant for inflating the truth, especially where it concerned him—were not as generous as Cowley. Joseph Conrad's wife denounced him to the *Times Literary Supplement* after Ford published a book claiming that Conrad had borrowed plot ideas from him. Her attack wounded Ford to the quick but did not stop him from bragging.

He was a gargantuan man with gargantuan needs. His appetite for women was apparently endless. Cowley remembered him, late in life, fondling young American women at a literary party. During his first marriage Ford had an affair with his wife's older sister. Later he filed for divorce, intending to marry a new lover, a woman 17 years his senior, but his wife sued for the "Restitution of Conjugal Rights," and her suit ruined Ford financially. For a time he had to write under a pseudonym in order to avoid his creditors.

His lust for literary greatness was just as extreme. A brilliant editor who numbered among his protegés D. H. Lawrence, Ezra Pound, and James Joyce, Ford wanted nothing less than to be a master novelist himself. He ranked his work on a par with that of his idol, Henry James.

It was James who inspired Ford's one universally acknowledged masterpiece, *The Good Soldier*. Ford finished the book in 1914, the same year he published a critical study of Henry James's fiction. His reading of James's novels had led him to write his finest, most complex and compelling narrative.

Ford initially titled his novel *The Saddest Story*, but his publisher, noting that such a title might deter sales in World War I England, convinced him to adopt the more patriotic *The Good Soldier*.

Although the book received mixed reviews when it appeared in 1915, *The Good Soldier* has since earned a place among the masterworks of modern fiction. Ironically, Ford himself did not live to see his reputation soar. Only in death has he achieved the renown to which he laid claim—so often and so loudly—during his life.

Shirley Jackson, b. 1919

Maxwell Anderson, b. 1888

Jane Austen, b. 1775
Noel Coward, b. 1899

Ford Madox Ford, b. 1873

H.H. Munro (Saki), b. 1870

Jean Genet, b. 1910

November						
S	M	T	W	T	F	S
						1
2	3	4	5	6	7	8
9	10	11	12	13	14	15
16	17	18	19	20	21	22
23	24	25	26	27	28	29
30						

December
1997

January 1998						
S	M	T	W	T	F	S
				1	2	3
4	5	6	7	8	9	10
11	12	13	14	15	16	17
18	19	20	21	22	23	24
25	26	27	28	29	30	31

Sunday
21

Winter Solstice, 3:09 pm EST

Monday
22

Tuesday
23

Giuseppe di Lampedusa, b. 1896
Chanukkah begins at sunset

Wednesday
24

Juan Ramón Jiménez, b. 1881
Matthew Arnold, b. 1822

Thursday
25

Christmas Day

Friday
26

Jean Toomer, b. 1894
Henry Miller, b. 1891
Boxing Day
Kwanzaa

Saturday
27

		November				
S	M	T	W	T	F	S
						1
2	3	4	5	6	7	8
9	10	11	12	13	14	15
16	17	18	19	20	21	22
23	24	25	26	27	28	29
30						

December
1997

		January 1998				
S	M	T	W	T	F	S
				1	2	3
4	5	6	7	8	9	10
11	12	13	14	15	16	17
18	19	20	21	22	23	24
25	26	27	28	29	30	31

Henry Miller
(December 26, 1891 - June 7, 1980)

He grew up in Brooklyn in a flat over a barber-shop. Both his father and his grandfather were tailors. "Every member of our family did something with his hands," Henry Miller said. "I'm the first son of a bitch with a glib tongue and a bad heart."

At the public library, Miller read voraciously and indiscriminately—Emerson, Whitman, Rabelais, unabridged dictionaries. The sound and the sense of unusual words intrigued him, and he filled notebooks with word lists and quotations from the books he read.

He studied literature at City College, but left after six weeks, defeated, he said, by Spenser's *Faerie Queen*. After years of working at various jobs, including stints as a ranch hand, an employment manager at Western Union, and the operator of a speakeasy, Miller traveled to Paris in 1928 and fell in love with the city. In 1930, he moved there and for the next nine years Paris became "mother, mistress, home and muse."

He found his way as a writer in Paris. Equipped with an engaging Brooklyn accent, a ribald sense of humor, an intense love for literature, and boundless enthusiasm, Miller charmed friends and acquaintances who loaned him money, clothes, and living quarters. "Only get desperate enough and everything will turn out well" was his motto. He wrote autobiographically in the first person and worked at a typewriter, playing it like a piano because he liked the sound it made.

In September 1934, *Tropic of Cancer*, his first book, was published in Paris. "At last an unprintable book that is fit to read," said Ezra Pound. United States Customs banned the book, and the restriction was not lifted until 1964, when the Supreme Court decided that the ban was unconstitutional. "Don't bother to fight for my books," Miller wrote Anaïs Nin. "I can bide my time."

Miller compared the process of writing a book to that of a snake shedding its skin. "The important book, the new skin, is always the one that is unborn." Books, includ-ing *Tropic of Capricorn, Black Spring, The Colossus of Maroussi*, essays, articles, and letters leapt out of Miller's typewriter. H. L. Mencken called his prose style beautiful.

In 1975 the French government awarded him the Legion of Honor. While American honors eluded him, Miller inspired Jack Kerouac and other writers of the Beat Generation. Sex and obscenity were necessary in literature, Miller believed, but he opposed pornography, the prurient use of sex. "Whatever I do is done out of sheer joy," he said. "I drop my fruits like a ripe tree."

The Editor

Writers are full of advice on what an editor should and should not do. To James Thurber, the best editor was the one who "edits least all things, especially mine." John Cheever defined a good editor as a man who was charming and who sent him large checks, praised his work, his beauty, and his sexual prowess, "and who has a stranglehold on the publisher and the bank."

Traditionally, a writer's most important and enduring literary relationship has been with his or her editor. Thomas Wolfe said once to Maxwell Perkins, his editor at Scribner's, "You are one of the rocks to which my life is anchored."

New Yorker editor Katharine White: "a velvet hand in an iron glove"

Dashiell Hammet sent telegram after telegram to his editor, Alfred Knopf, Sr., requesting advances for books which he promised to write. Ever hopeful, Knopf obliged him. But he was skeptical. "I'm damned if one of these days I don't wire you to deposit X dollars for me in my bank account as an advance against the profits that ought to accrue to me and would if you'd do your duty by us," he complained to Hammett in 1935. A few months later, Hammett wired Knopf for more money.

Not all writers enjoy such editorial pampering. When Karl Marx was ten months late with his manuscript for *Das Kapital*, his publisher in Leipzig warned, "If we do not receive the manuscript within six months, we shall be obliged to commission another to do this work."

During her 35 years at the *New Yorker*, Katharine White edited Vladimir Nabokov, John O'Hara, May Sarton, Nadine Gordimer, and many others with a firm, loving, and meticulous hand. Should the color be written "grey" or "gray"? asked Mary McCarthy. The magazine preferred "gray." Katharine and McCarthy agreed that the use "depended on what shade one meant." "Grey" seemed lighter to both women.

A good editor anticipates critical assaults and protects the writer from the sin of pride. "It is advantageous to an author," said Samuel Johnson, "that his book should be attacked as well as praised. Fame is a shuttlecock. If it be struck at only one end of the room, it will soon fall to the ground. To keep it up, it must be struck at both ends."

From his editors at the *New Yorker*, Irwin Shaw learned "the value of cutting out the last paragraph of stories, something I pass down as a tip to all writers. The last paragraph in which you tell what the story is about is almost always best left out."

Sunday
28

 Monday
29

Tuesday
30

Wednesday
31

Ramadan begins

Thursday
1

Catherine Drinker Bowen, b. 1897   New Year's Day

Friday
2

Saturday
3

November
S	M	T	W	T	F	S
						1
2	3	4	5	6	7	8
9	10	11	12	13	14	15
16	17	18	19	20	21	22
23	24	25	26	27	28	29
30						

December/January
1997/1998

January 1998
S	M	T	W	T	F	S
				1	2	3
4	5	6	7	8	9	10
11	12	13	14	15	16	17
18	19	20	21	22	23	24
25	26	27	28	29	30	31

Bibliography

Asquith, Cynthia. *Portrait of Barrie*. New York: E. P. Dutton and Co., 1955.

Atkinson, Brooks. *Broadway*. New York: Limelight Editions, 1970.

Berendsohn, Walter A. *Selma Lagerlöf. Her Life and Work*. Adapted from the German by George F. Timpson. With a preface by Vita Sackville-West. Port Washington, N.Y.: Kennikat Press, Inc., 1931.

Bernstein, Richard. "Howard's Way." *The New York Times Magazine*. September 25, 1988. Pages 40-92.

Bernstein, Burton. *Thurber*. New York: Dodd, Mead and Company, 1975.

Birkin, Andrew. *J. M. Barrie and The Lost Boys*. New York: Clarkson N. Potter, Inc., 1979.

Bissinger, H. G. "Main Line Madcap." *Vanity Fair*. October 1995. Pages 158-182.

Blythe, Ronald. "Anaïs Nin." *The Pleasures of Diaries. Four Centuries of Private Writing*. Selected by Ronald Blythe. New York: Pantheon, 1989.

Brady, Frank. *James Boswell: The Later Years*. New York: McGraw-Hill Book Company, 1984.

Broyard, Anatole. "Good Books About Being Sick." *The New York Times Book Review*. April 1, 1990.

Camus, Albert. *Notebooks. 1942-1951*. Translated from the French and annotated by Justin O'Brien. New York: Alfred A. Knopf, 1965.

Carpenter, Margaret Haley. *Sara Teasdale. A Biography*. New York: Schulte Publishing Company, 1960.

Castro, Rosalía de. *Poesía*. Traducción, selección y prólogo de Mauro Armiño. Madrid: Alianza Editorial, 1986.

Charlton, James, ed. *Fighting Words*. Chapel Hill: Algonquin Books, 1994.

Charvet, P. E. *A Literary History of France. Volume IV. The Nineteenth Century. 1789-1870*. London: Ernest Benn Limited, 1967.

Chute, Marchette. *Ben Jonson of Westminster*. New York: E. P. Dutton and Co., 1953.

Cook, Blanche Wiesen. *Eleanor Roosevelt. Volume One. 1884-1933*. New York: Viking, 1992.

Davis, Linda H. *Onward and Upward. A Biography of Katharine S. White*. New York: Harper and Row, 1987.

Dennis, Nigel. *Jonathan Swift*. New York: The Macmillan Company, 1964.

Dettelbach, Cynthia Golomb. *In the Driver's Seat. The Automobile in American Literature and Popular Culture*. Westport, Ct.: Greenwood Press, 1976.

Dickson, Lovat. *H. G. Wells: His Turbulent Life and Times*. New York: Atheneum, 1969.

Eliot, T. S. "Andrew Marvell." In *Selected Essays*. New Edition. New York: Harcourt, Brace and World, Inc., 1964. Pages 251-263.

Engen, Rodney. *Kate Greenaway. A Biography*. London: Macdonald Futura Publishers, 1981.

Gennimore, Keith J. *Booth Tarkington*. New York: Twayne Publishers, 1974.

Foley, Helene P., ed. *Reflections of Women in Antiquity*. New York: Gordon and Breach Science Publishers, 1981.

Fjelde, Rolf. "Lost in Translation." *Theatre Communications*. Vol. 6, No. 2. February 1984. Pages 1-4.

Frank, Elizabeth. *Louise Bogan. A Portrait*. New York: Columbia University Press, 1986.

Gordon, Lyndall. *Virginia Woolf. A Writer's Life*. New York: Norton, 1984.

Griffith, Elisabeth. *In Her Own Right. The Life of Elizabeth Cady Stanton*. New York: Oxford University Press, 1984.

Grossman, James. *James Fenimore Cooper*. New York: William Sloane Associates, 1949.

Gruber, Frank. *Horatio Alger, Jr. A Biography and Bibliography*. Los Angeles: Grover Jones Press, 1961.

Hanson, Bruce. *The Peter Pan Chronicles*. New York: Birch Lane Press, 1993.

"*Heidi*—or the Story of A Juvenile Best Seller." *Publishers' Weekly*. July 25, 1953.

Heffernan, James A. W., ed. *Representing the French Revolution. Literature, Historiography, and Art*. Hanover, N. H.: Dartmouth College, 1992.

Henry Miller Letters to Anaïs Nin. Edited and with an introduction by Gunther Stuhlmann. New York: G. P. Putnam's Sons, 1965.

Holmes, William, and Edward Mitchel, eds. *Nineteenth-Century American Short Fiction*. New York: Scott, Foresman, 1970.

Johnson, Diane. *Dashiell Hammett. A Life*. New York: Random House, 1983.

Kaplan, Fred. *Dickens*. New York: William Morrow and Company, 1988.

Kaplan, Justin. *Mr. Clemens and Mark Twain*. New York: Simon and Schuster, 1966.

Lagerlöf, Selma. *The Diary of Selma Lagerlöf*. Translated by Velma Swanston Howard. New York: Doubleday, 1936. Reprinted by Kraus Repring Co., Millwood, New York, 1975.

Lash, Joseph H. *Eleanor and Franklin*. New York: W. W. Norton and Company, 1971.

Levine, Philip. "Living in Machado." In *The Bread of Time. Towards an Autobiography*. New York: Alfred A. Knopf, 1994.

Lewis, R. W. B. *Edith Wharton*. New York: Fromm International Publishing Corporation, 1985.

Lottman, Herbert R. *Albert Camus*. Garden City, New York: Doubleday and Company, 1979.

Marvell, Andrew. *The Essential Marvell*. Selected and with an introduction by Donald Hall. New York: The Ecco Press, 1991.

May, Derwent. *Hannah Arendt*. New York: Viking Penguin, 1986.

Methley, Violet. *Camille Desmoulins. A Biography*. London: Martin Secker, 1915.

Morante, Elsa. *Opere*. A cura di Carlo Cecchi e Cesare Garboli. Volume primo. Milano: Arnoldo Mondadori, 1988.

Older, Julia. "Poeming a Translation." *Poets and Writers Magazine*. July/August 1994. Pages 27-31.

Oppenheimer, George, ed. *The Passionate Playgoer*. New York: The Viking Press, 1958.

Pasternak, Boris. *The Voice of Prose*. Edited by Christopher Barnes. New York: Grove Press, 1986.

Paton, Alan. *Journey Continued*. New York: Charles Scribner's Sons, 1980.

_____. *Towards the Mountain*. New York: Charles Scribner's Sons, 1980.

Plimpton, George, ed. *The Writer's Chapbook. A Compendium of Fact, Opinion, Wit, and Advice from the 20th Century's Preeminent Writers*. New York: Viking, 1990.

The Poems of Sappho. Translated, with an introduction, by Suzy Q. Groden. New York: The Bobbs-Merrill Company, 1966.

Raper, Julius Rowan, ed. *Ellen Glasgow's Reasonable Doubts. A Collection of Her Writings*. Baton Rouge and London: Louisiana State University Press, 1988.

Ray, Gordon N. *H. G. Wells and Rebecca West*. New Haven: Yale University Press, 1974.

Rinehart, Mary Roberts. *My Story*. New York: Rinehart and Company, Inc., 1931.

Roethke, Theodore. "What Do I Like?" In *The Structure of Verse. Modern Essays on Prosody*. Edited with an introduction and commentary by Harvey Gross. Revised edition. New York: The Ecco Press, 1979.

Rouse, Blair. *Ellen Glasgow*. New York: Twayne Publishers, 1962.

Russell, John. "The Smallest Museum in Russia: Akhmatova Lived Here (and Lives Here Still)." *The New York Times Book Review*. January 1, 1995.

Sandblom, Philip. *Creativity and Disease. How Illness Affects Literature, Art and Music*. Philadelphia: George F. Stickley Company, 1982.

Schama, Simon. *Citizens. A Chronicle of the French Revolution*. New York: Alfred A. Knopf, 1989.

Schifano, Jean-Noël, and Tjuna Notarbartolo. *Cahiers Elsa Morante*. Napoli: Edizioni Scientifiche Italiene, 1993.

Schoen, Carol B. *Sara Teasdale*. Boston: Twayne Publishers, 1986.

Specter, Michael. "St. Petersburg Journal. If Poet's Room Could Speak, It Would Tell of Grief." *The New York Times*. June 28, 1995.

Steele, Zulma. "Fannie Farmer and Her Cook Book." In Leon Stein, ed., *Lives to Remember*. New York: Arno Press, 1974. Pages 66-71.

Stevens, Shelley. *Rosalía de Castro and the Galician Revival*. London: Tamesis Books, 1986.

Thiebaux, Marcelle. *Ellen Glasgow*. New York: Frederick Ungar Publishing Co., 1982.

Thurber, James. "He Edits Best Who Edits Least All Things, Especially Mine." *The New York Times Book Review*. December 4, 1988. Pages 7, 44.

Tinker, Chauncey Brewster. *Young Boswell*. Boston: The Atlantic Monthly Press, 1922.

Ueda, Makoto. *Matsuo Bashō*. New York: Kodansha International, 1982.

Washington, Mary Helen. *Invented Lives. Narratives of Black Women 1860-1960*. New York: Anchor Press, 1987.

Winslow, Kathryn. *Henry Miller: Full of Life*. New York: St. Martin's Press, 1986.

Wright, Constance. *Fanny Kemble and the Lovely Land*. New York: Dodd, Mead and Company, 1972.

Photo And Illustration Credits

Many of the photographs reproduced in this book come from the collections of the Library of Congress, Washington, D.C.

The authors wish to acknowledge the following additional sources of photographs and illustrations:

Hannah Arendt: UPI/Bettmann

J.M. Barrie: The Hulton Deutsch Collection

Matsuo Bashō: *Portrait of the Poet Bashō* by Yokoi Kinkoku (Japanese, 1761-1832), The University of Michigan Museum of Art, Margaret Watson Parker Art Collection 1968/2.22

James Boswell: The Hulton Deutsch Collection

Antoine de Saint Exupéry: UPI/Bettmann

Ford Maddox Ford: The Hulton Deutsch Collection

Ben Jonson: The Hulton Deutsch Collection

Selma Lagerlöf: The Bettmann Archive

Andrew Marvell: The Hulton Deutsch Collection

Henry Miller: UPI/Bettmann

Elsa Morante: Jerry Bauer/Random House

Anaïs Nin: UPI/Bettmann

Boris Pasternak: UPI/Bettmann

Alan Paton: UPI/Bettmann

Theodore Roethke: UPI/Bettmann

Eleanor Roosevelt: UPI/Bettmann

Sappho: UPI/Bettmann

Jonathan Swift: The Hulton Deutsch Collection

Sara Teasdale: UPI/Bettmann

James Thurber: UPI/Bettmann

Katharine White: Linda Davis

About the Authors

The authors of "On Writers and Writing" are both biographers. Helen Sheehy is the author of *Margo: The Life and Theatre of Margo Jones*, (Southern Methodist University, 1989) and *Eva Le Gallienne* (Alfred A. Knopf, 1996). A resident of Connecticut, Sheehy has written a theater textbook, a number of articles and essays, and has taught theater for over twenty years.

Leslie Stainton lives in Michigan and is at work on a biography of Federico Garcia Lorca for which she received a two-year Fulbright Research Grant. Her articles and essays have appeared in various newspapers and periodicals including the *New York Times,* the *Washington Post*, and *American Theatre* magazine.